PRO
GU
SCALE PATTERNS

...A VISUAL APPROACH
TO THE SCALES
MOST COMMONLY USED
IN JAZZ, ROCK AND
BLUES

by DON LATARSKI

Photo: Brian Lanker

About the author...

Don Latarski has been playing the guitar since 1963. He's an adjunct faculty member at the University of Oregon's Music School. In addition to this book, he's written a number of others on guitar instruction: *Introduction to Chord Theory, Moveable Guitar Chords, Scale Patterns for Guitar, Arpeggios for Guitar* and *Chord Embesllshment.* Known nationally as a a gifted guitarist and composer; Don performs frequently with his group at Jazz Festivals and Clubs in the Pacific Northwest. His music can be heard on "HAVEN", Inner City Records and "LIFELINE", PAUSA Records. Originally a Michigan native, Don has made Eugene, Oregon his home since 1973 where he builds and rides recumbant bicycles when it's not raining.

TABLE OF CONTENTS

INTRODUCTION

Every aspiring improviser needs a wide variety of scales to draw on. It's no longer enough for a rock guitarist to know just the "rock scale" (see minor pentatonic). Contemporary rock guitarists are now using the modes of the major scale, blues scales, diminished scales, whole tone scales and a host of others. In the never-ending quest for a personal sound, guitarists have embraced all sorts of exotic scale sounds.

This book is a collection of the most common scales used by improvisers. Many of the scales found here are used frequently by jazz musicians, who need a large number of scales due to the harmonic complexity of this style.

In the beginning, God created the chromatic scale (among others), which contains every possible scale which we as "Westerners" have seen fit to invent. The chromatic scale is made up of twelve different pitches, each a half-step (the smallest musical distance between any two notes. Other cultures commonly use smaller intervals in their scales.) apart. Starting from C, this scale would have the following pitches: C-C#-D-D#-E-F-F#-G-G#-A-A#-B. Every scale or mode in this book is made up of some combination of these pitches.

I'm a firm believer in fretboard visualization. The layout of the scales reflects this belief. I show each scale or mode in a number of different ways: The first way involves showing the scale formula. The scale formula tells you how a scale or mode deviates from a major scale. Everything in music theory is based on the major scale and how it deviates from it. For example, the scale formula for a major scale is: 1-2-3-4-5-6-7. If we use C as our beginning note, the C major scale is: C-D-E-F-G-A-B. In the key of A major, the notes would be: A-B-C#-D-E-F#-G#. (see the appendix for all of the major scales.) The formula for A major is still 1-2-3-4-5-6-7. Confused? There's another way of describing the major scale. We can do it by looking at how far the notes are apart. This brings us back to the idea of intervals. In every major scale, the distance between the 1st and 2nd notes is a whole-step. In fact, the distance between most notes in a major scale is a whole step. The half-steps occur between the 3rd and 4th scales degrees and the 7th and 8th. This relationship is expressed with the formula: 1-2-3-4-5-6-7.

W=whole step   W W h W W W h
h=half step   1 - 2 - 3 - 4 - 5 - 6 - 7 - 8

A scale that has a formula such as: 1-2-b3-4-5-b6-b7, is one that has three notes which are different than the major scale version of this scale. We'd describe this scale as having a flatted 3rd, 6th and 7th. The name given to this scale is Natural Minor.

It is actually possible to visualize on the fingerboard using the idea of 1-2-3-4-5-6-7. It's not obvious, like a fingering pattern. But every fingering pattern can be translated into a set of numbers like the ones above.

The next method I use to show a scale is with traditional notation. In most cases, I've based the scale root (the starting note) on G. For those of you who can't read, it's not necessary to know what these pitches are. What is important is that you learn to define a scale or mode sound by its formula. Also, isn't this a great time to get some reading chops together?

The next way I use to show a scale involves actually mapping the scale out over the entire fingerboard. I came across this idea many years ago when I was trying to teach myself every possible way to play a major scale. I simply took every note in the C major scale and drew a dot on the fingerboard on every C-D-E-F-G-A-B. I then tried to break this chaotic group of dots into small fingering patterns. These smaller patterns are the ones shown on the right hand side of the page. (I've bracketed the left hand side page to show you where I broke out the various patterns found on the right hand side of the page.) I found that by linking these smaller patterns together, I could span the entire fingerboard. Notice also that there is always some overlapping that goes on between each of these smaller patterns. These are the notes which you can use to slide from one pattern to the next.

Some of you may have even done what I've just described for yourself and come up with entirely different fingering patterns. This is entirely possible and equally valid. My goal in coming up with my fingerings was to find patterns which didn't involve large hand spreads. Some folks prefer other types of patterns. You may want to work out some of your own patterns. It's a great way to assume responsibility for your own learning.

All scales and modes are accompanied with a brief example as to how you might apply it. Any given scale or mode has a root note. This is the first note of the scale. A primary application of a scale would be where the root note of the scale is G and the root note of the chord we want to use it with is also G. As an example, a G major scale would sound great when played over a G major 7th chord. There are other less obvious applications of scales. These uses I call secondary. An example of a secondary use would be using a D major scale over a G major 7th chord. This does actually work. It produces a Lydian type sound. In secondary applications of the scales and modes, the root tone of the scale does not correspond to the root tone of the chord over which the scale is being used.

The solid colored dots on the fingerboard will all show the location of the scale or mode root. In most cases, these notes will all be G's. These notes are highlighted because they are the most important tones in the scale. The location of the root tones within any fingering pattern affect the phrasing and fingering choices. Our ears also use the root to define any given scale or mode sound.

In this book, the term mode and scale are used interchangeably. Modes are actually derived from scales. In a stricter sense, the term mode dates back to the medieval church modes. During this time, it became common practice to construct a scale (mode) from the tones of the major scale, which usually began and ended on one of the tones in the scale other than the tonic (root note)of the key. This is easily accomplished by simply taking the second note of the major scale and calling it the new root tone of the new scale. Thus, the second mode of the major scale of C is composed of the following notes: D-E-F-G-A-B-C. This is the Dorian mode. The formula for it is: 1-2-b3-4-5-6-b7. It has a minor type sound because of the lowered 3rd and 7th.

It's possible to construct a mode on any note of any scale, be it from the Harmonic minor, Diminished, Melodic minor or Pentatonic scales. The reason for learning these modes is simple; by manipulating these pitches, you can get some very interesting sounds.

HOW TO USE THIS BOOK

When learning a new scale, begin by studying and practicing the individual patterns. Pay particular attention to the root notes in each of the patterns. I usually start by playing about half of the pattern. This spans an octave. I also strongly urge you to record a chord which can sound while you're trying to get the scale in your fingers. You need to be training your ear as well as your fingers when learning new scale and mode sounds.If you're going to practice the Dorian sound, put down some min6, min7, min9 and min11 chords on tape or program them into your sequencer. (If your going for the C Dorian mode, make sure all of the roots to the above chords are also C.)

I always learn how to play the finger pattern across the fingerboard, then I start connecting two patterns; running back and forth from one to the other, working out appropriate finger shifts. Then I begin building runs that span 3 or more patterns. I also always try to be musical when the guitar is in my hands. This goes for practicing scales too. I play them with feeling and intent. I don't sit in front of the TV and practice. I concentrate on what I'm doing and do it intensely for short periods of time.

There are always alternate ways of fingering anything and this goes for scales too. You may find a number of alternate fingerings. Explore them all. Different fingerings will result in new musical ideas. Play these scales in any way you can imagine. Experiment with different rhythmic groupings such as eighth notes, sixteenth notes, triplets and the like. There are many different exercises you can invent which will promote facility with the patterns. Playing the patterns in 3rd's, 4th's, 5th's and 6th's is also a good way to develop some new ideas as well as your crosspicking chops.

The biggest challenge to scale playing is bridging the gap between scales and music. All to often, the playing of scales turns into a boring exercise, where the student tries to divorce his/her brain from what the fingers are doing. This is mindless practicing and might even be a waste of time. The real danger here lies in the fact that you might be having a very negative experience with something that should be uplifting and positive. This kind of experience does little to promote creativity and experimentation. When the scales become tedious and boring, stop and give yourself a break. Do something more enjoyable. Set a pace for yourself that is ambitious yet attainable.

Lastly, I suggest learning the major scale and its modes first. These are by far the most important patterns. Next, learn the blues and pentatonic scales if you're into Rock and Blues. If you're into Jazz, make sure you know the Melodic minor and Harmonic minor scale modes (in addition to the major scale and its modes as well as the blues scale) . You'll also find that the Diminished (both versions) and the Whole tone scale are helpful.

I hope you find this book useful. I certainly have. If you like the way I've organized the material in this book, you may find that my other books, *Introduction to Chord Theory, Moveable Guitar Chords, Arpeggios for Guitar, Chord Embellishment and Chord Orbits,* will also be helpful.

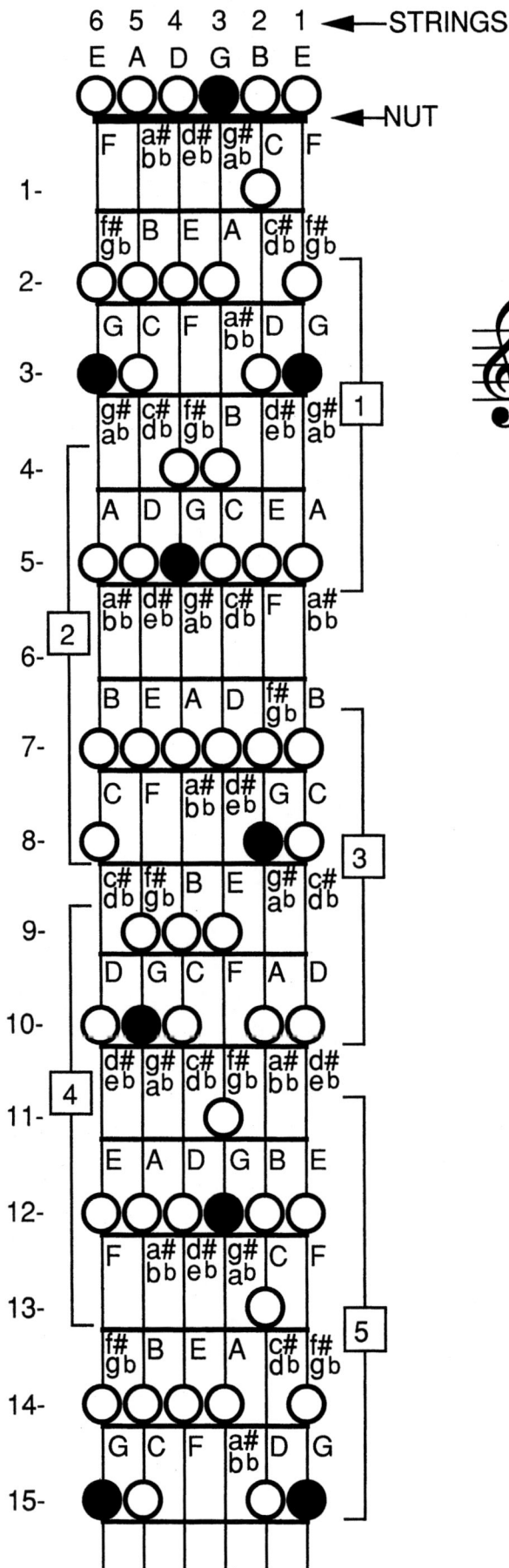

MAJOR/IONIAN

1-2-3-4-5-6-7

ALTERNATE NAMES:
The major scale is often called the Ionian mode.

PRIMARY USE:
The Ionian is used over unaltered maj type chords such as: maj. triads, maj6, maj7, maj6/9, maj9, maj6/7, maj add9. These chords are usually tonic functioning chords.

EXAMPLE:
Use the G Ionian for soloing over any of the above mentioned chords as long as their respective roots are all G notes.

IONIAN/major

1

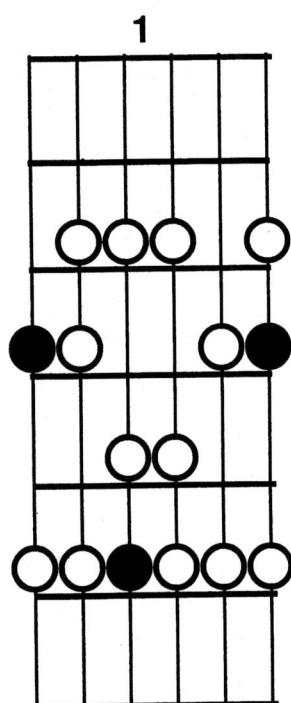

2

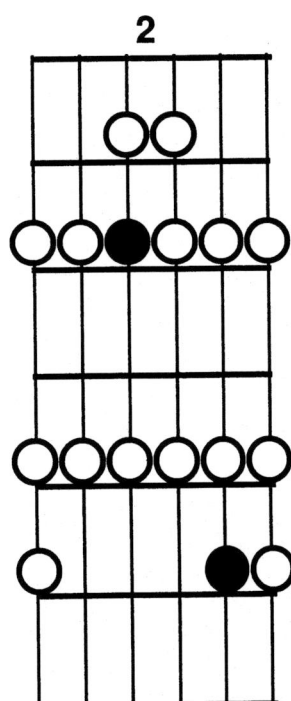

3

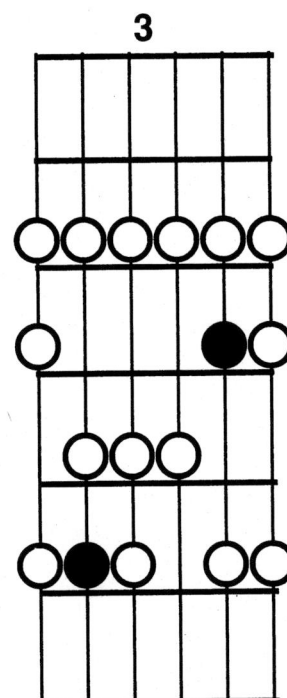

4

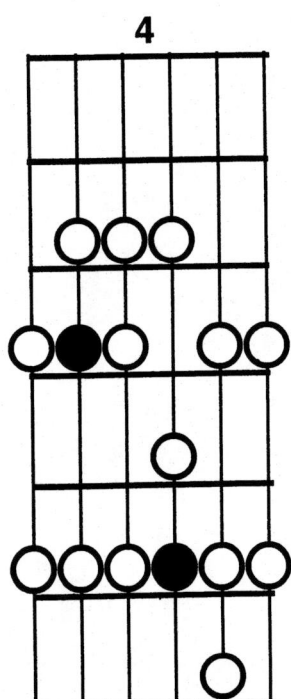

5

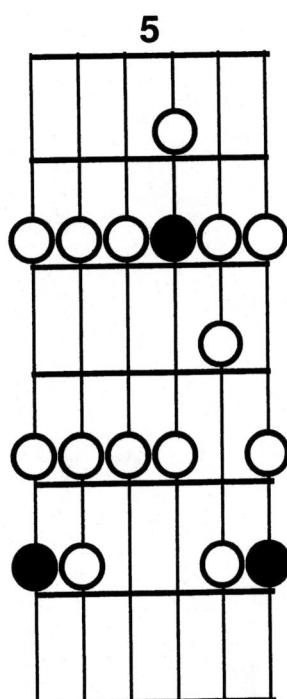

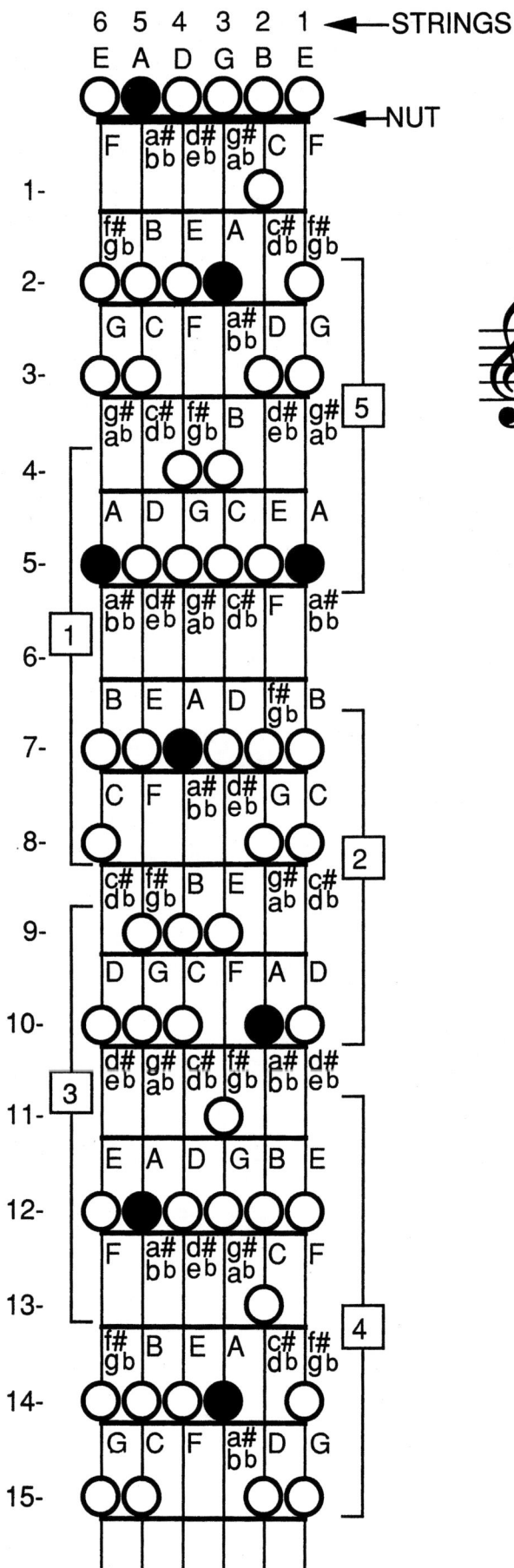

DORIAN

1-2-b3-4-5-6-b7

ALTERNATE NAMES:
none

PRIMARY USE:
This mode is used mostly over unaltered minor chords such as min. triads, min6, min6/9, min7, min9, min11, and min13. It can be used over tonic minor chords, but is most often heard over minor chords which function as a II chord.

EXAMPLE:
Use this A Dorian mode over any of the chords listed above which have A as their roots.

NOTE:
Some of you may have noticed that the patterns used for the A Dorian mode are the same as those used for G Ionian. The only difference between G Ionian and A Dorian is in the note of emphasis. In A Dorian, we want to orient (phrase from) to the A notes.

DORIAN

1

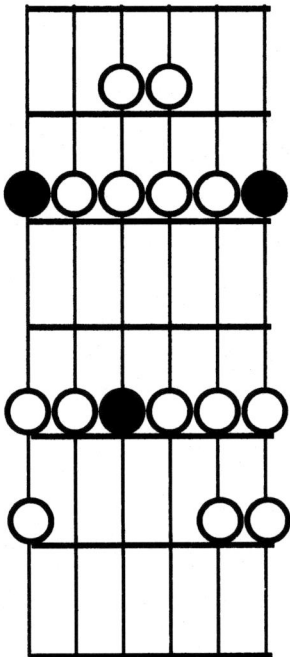

2

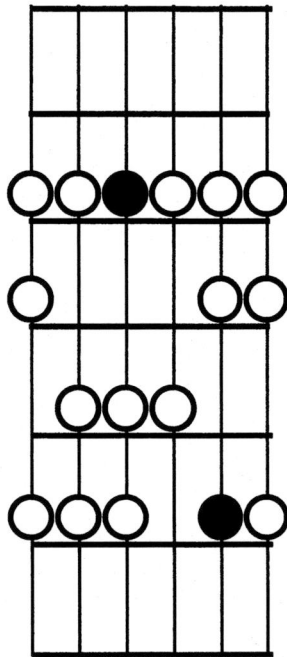

3

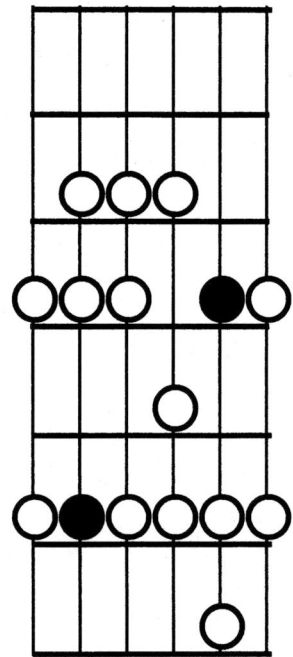

4

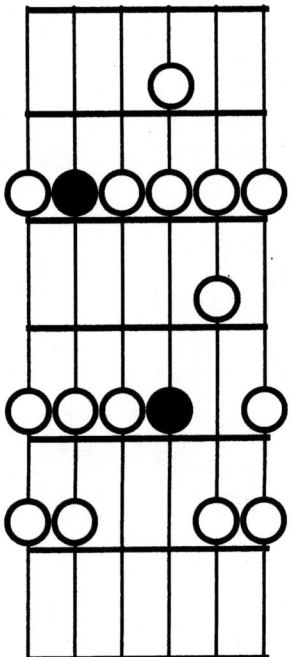

5

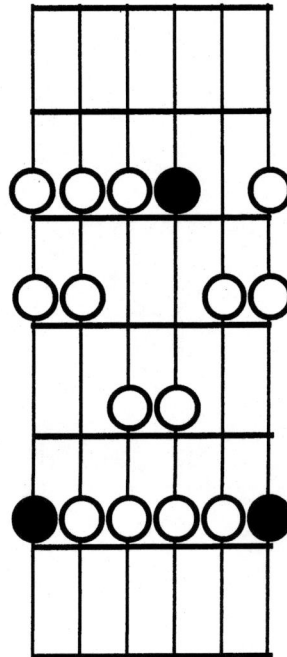

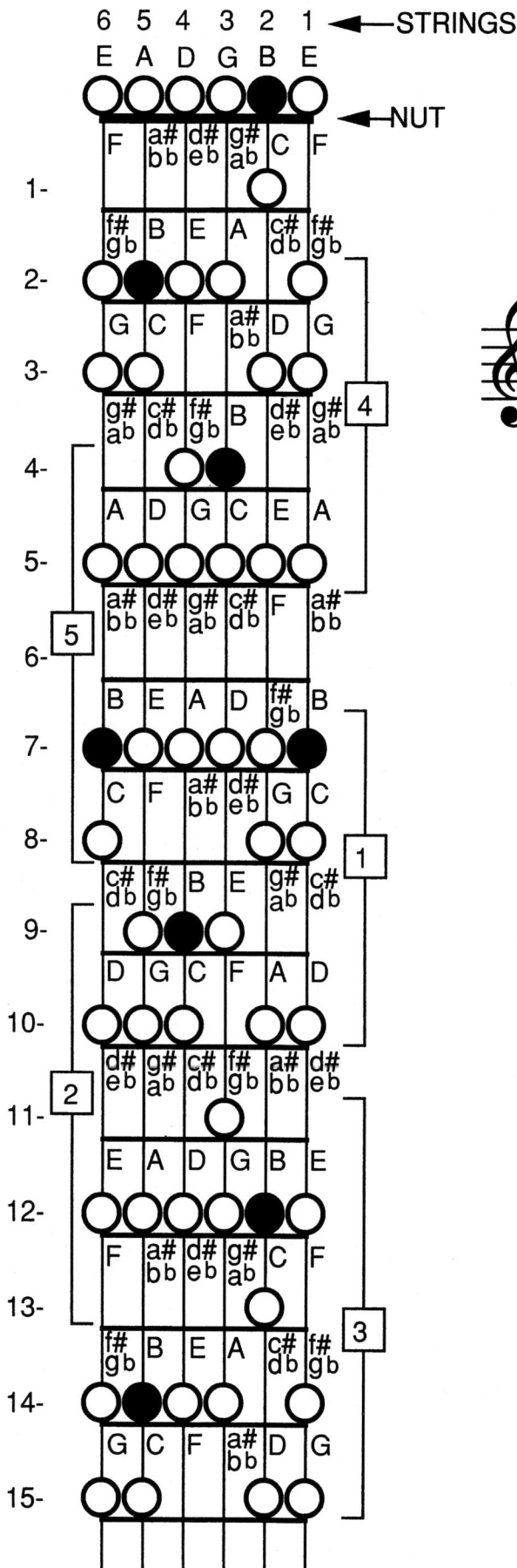

STRINGS

NUT

PHRYGIAN

1-b2-b3-4-5-b6-b7

ALTERNATE NAMES:

PRIMARY USE:

This mode is used over unaltered min chords such as a min7th. This chord is usually a III chord in the major key. It can also be used over a sus4, sus7 or major triad chord that is functioning as a tonic. This type of usage gives a spanish type flavor.

EXAMPLE:

Use this B Phrygin mode over any a Bm7 chord which is functioning as a III chord in major or over a B maj, Bsus4 or Bsus7 chord.

NOTE:

Some of you may have noticed that the patterns used for the A Dorian mode are the same as those used for B Phrygian. The only difference between A Dorian and B Phrygian is in the note of emphasis. In B Phrygian, we want to orient (phrase from) to the B notes.

PHRYGIAN

1

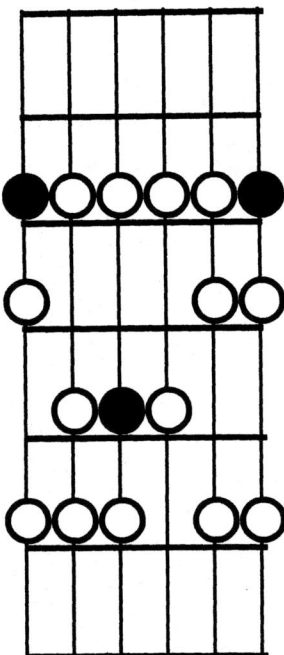

2

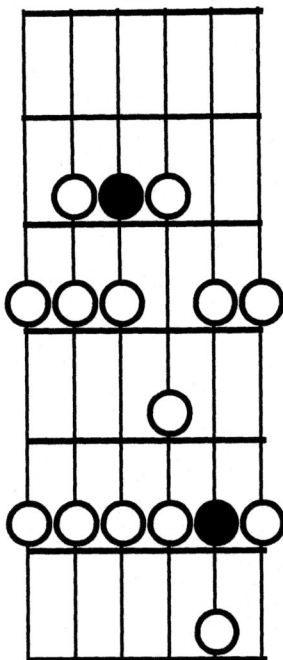

3

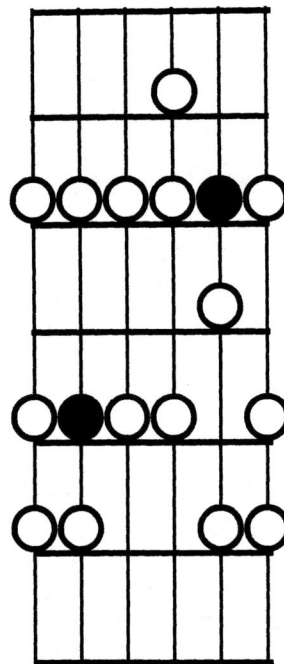

4

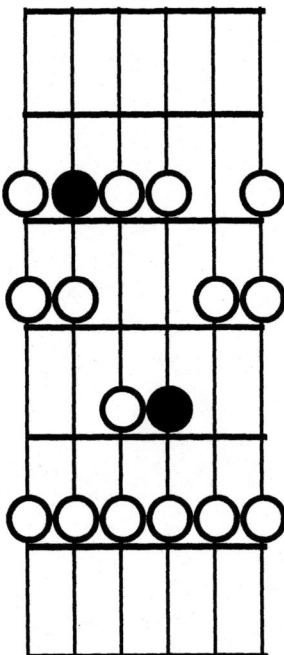

5

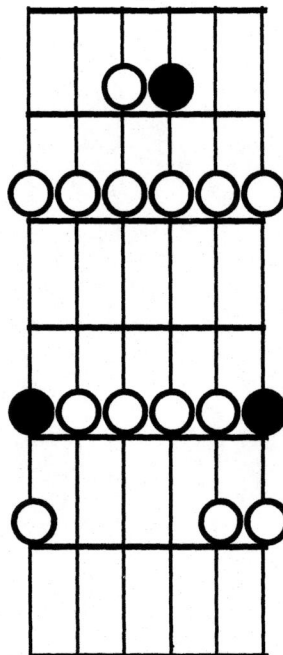

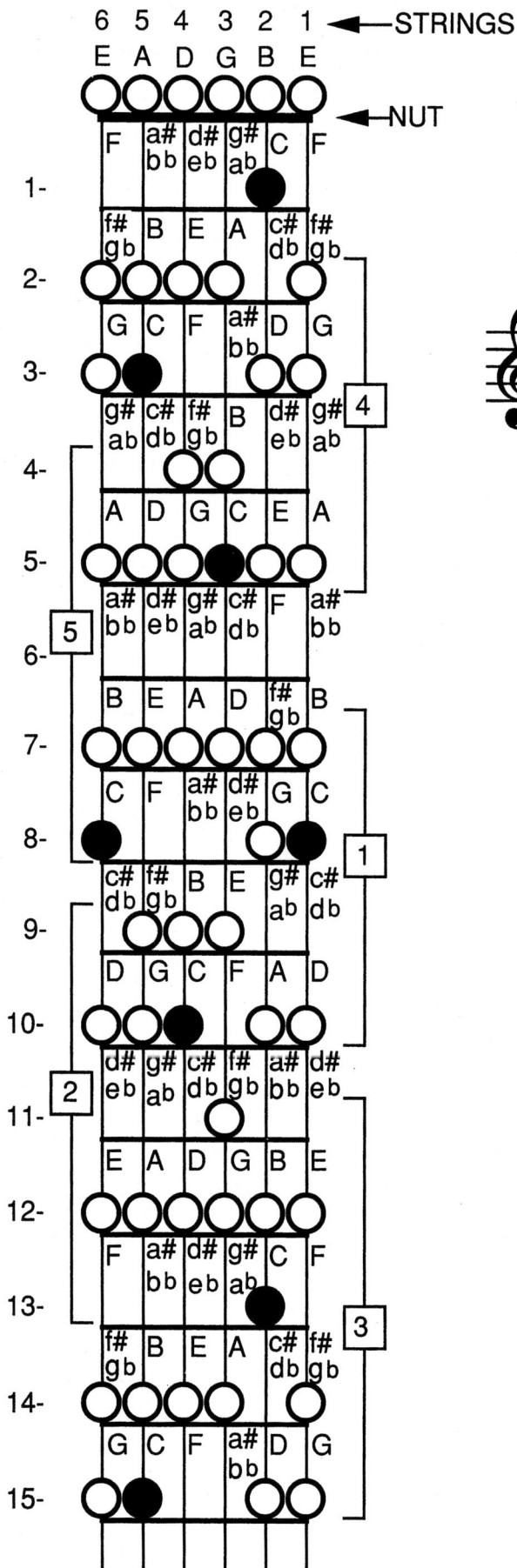

LYDIAN

1-2-3-#4-5-6-7

ALTERNATE NAMES:
none

PRIMARY USE:
This mode is used over major chords, especially maj7#4, maj7b5 and maj7#11 chords which are functioning as either I or IV chords in the major key. Many Jazz players use this scale where the Ionian would normally be used. Many people prefer the sound of Lydian over that of Ionian.

EXAMPLE:
Use this C Lydian mode over any maj chord especially Cmaj7#4, Cmaj7b5 and Cmaj7#11.

NOTE:
Some of you may have noticed that the patterns used for the B Phrygian mode are the same as those used for C Lydian. The only difference between B Bhrygian and C Lydian is in the note of emphasis. In C Lydian we want to orient (phrase from) to the C notes.

LYDIAN

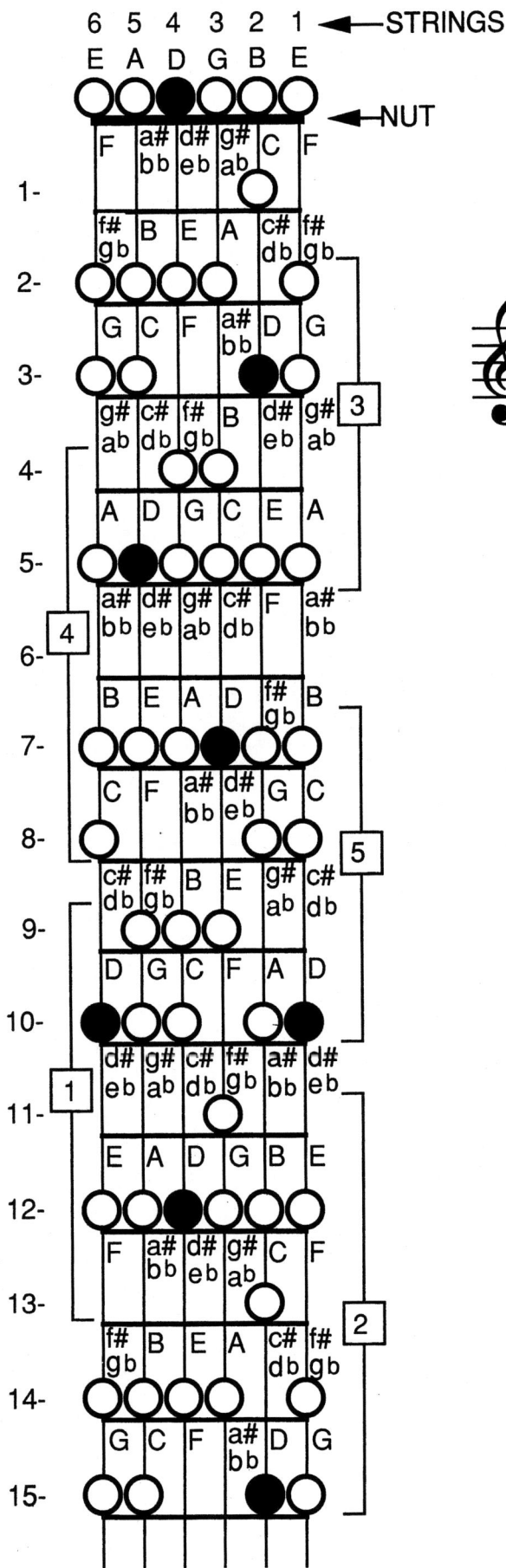

MIXOLYDIAN

1-2-3-4-5-6-b7

ALTERNATE NAMES:
none

PRIMARY USE:
This mode is used over unaltered dominant chords such as dom7, dom9, dom11, dom13 and sus4, sus7, sus9, and sus13 chords. This mode has a particularly bluesy sound and it can be used as a type of blues scale.

EXAMPLE:
Use this D mixolydian mode over D7, D9, D11, D13, Dsus4, Dsus7, Dsus9 and Dsus13.

NOTE:
Some of you may have noticed that the patterns used for the C Lydian mode are the same as those used for D Mixolydian. The only difference between C Phrygian and D Mixolydian is in the note of emphasis. In D Mixolydian we want to orient (phrase from) to the D notes.

MIXOLYDIAN

1

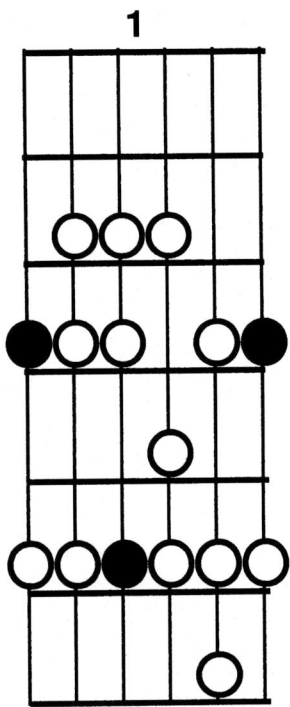

2

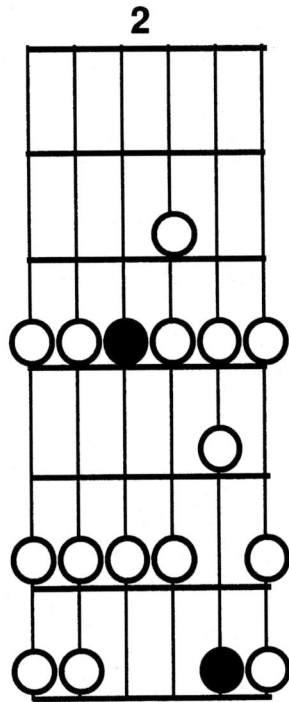

3

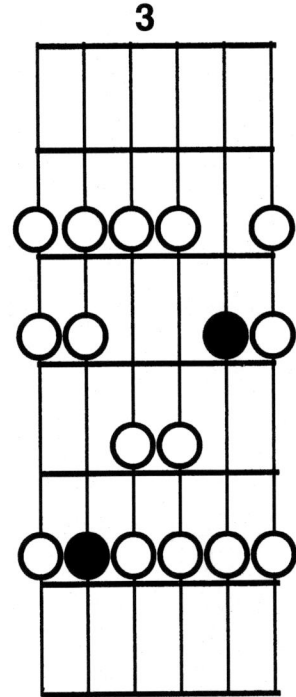

4

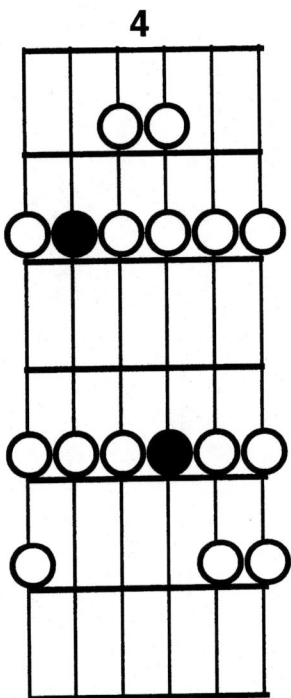

5

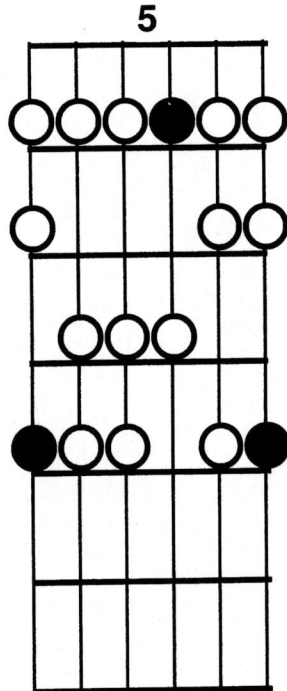

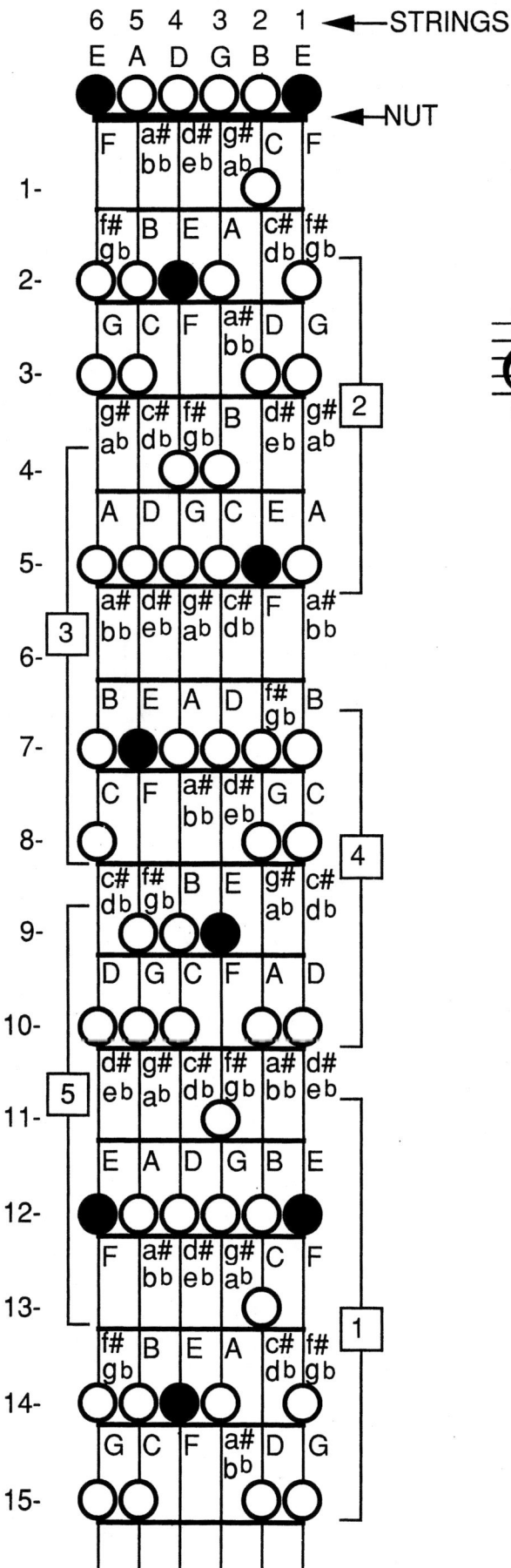

AEOLIAN

1-2-b3-4-5-b6-b7

ALTERNATE NAMES:

Natural Minor

PRIMARY USE:

This mode is used over min chords, especially min triads, min7, min7#5, min9 and min11 that are functioning as tonic chords. This mode doesn't work well with any minor chord which has a natural 6th such as min6, min6/9 and min13 chords.

EXAMPLE:

Use this E Aeolian mode over Em, Em7, Em7#5, Em9, and Em11.

NOTE:

Some of you may have noticed that the patterns used for the D Mixolydian mode are the same as those used for E Aeolian. The only difference between D Mixolydian and E Aeolian is in the note of emphasis. In E Aeolian we want to orient (phrase from) to the E notes.

AEOLIAN/natural minor

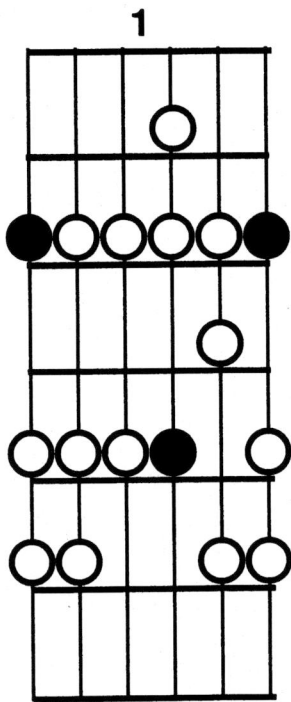

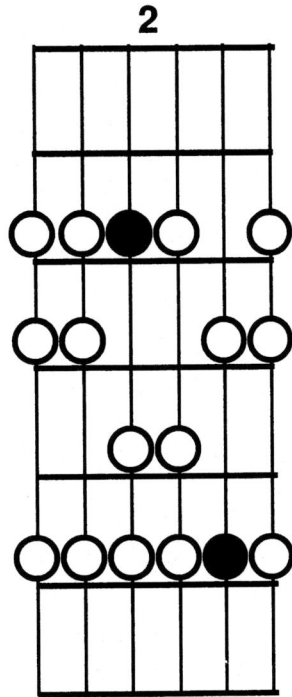

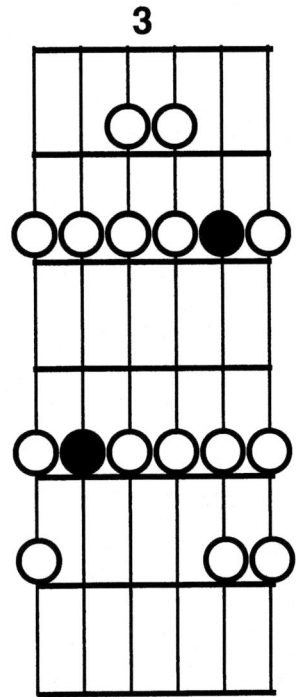

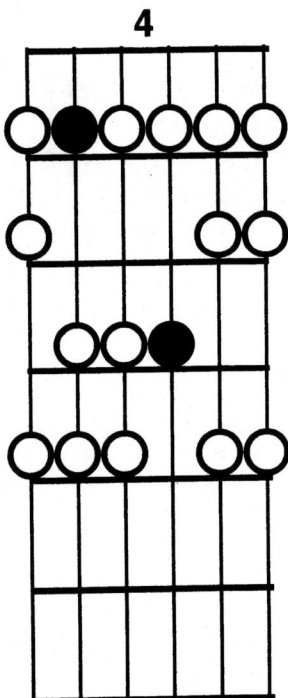

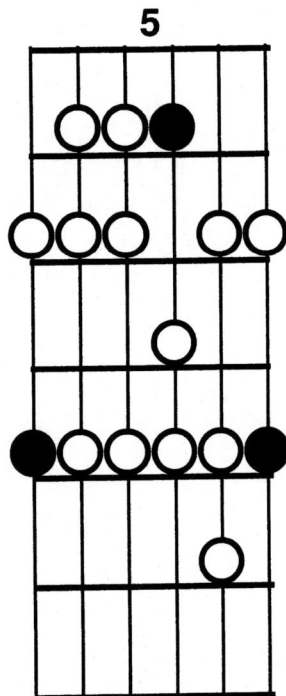

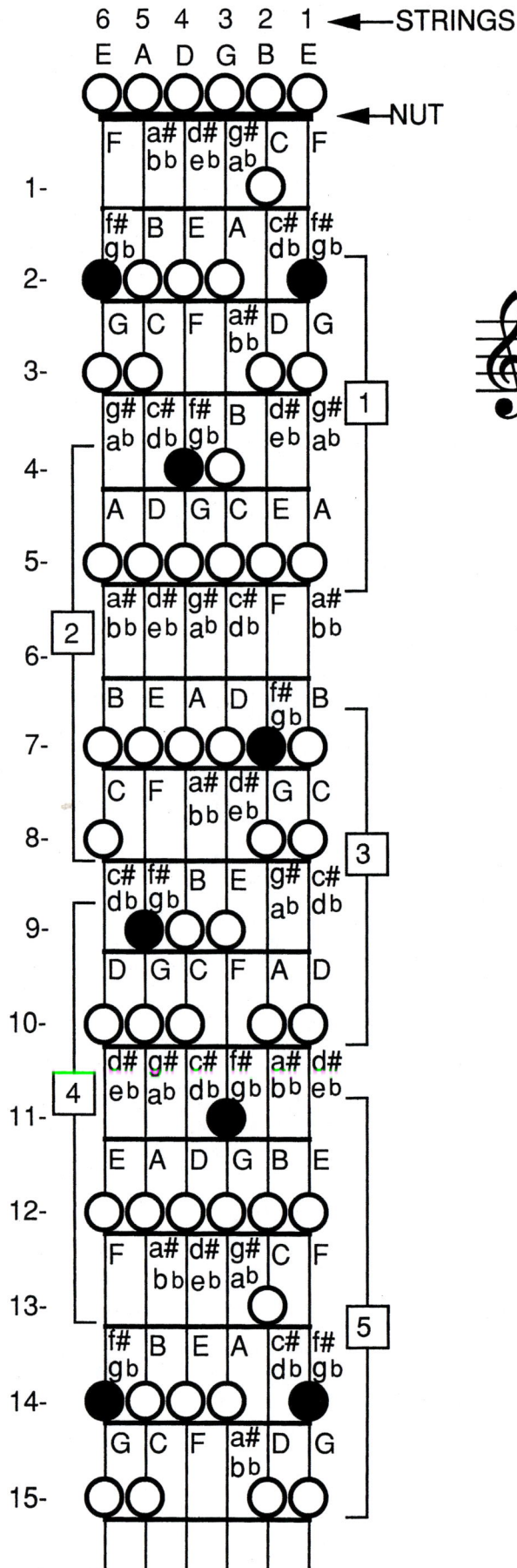

LOCRIAN

1-b2-b3-4-b5-b6-b7

ALTERNATE NAMES:
none

PRIMARY USE:
This mode is used over min7b5 chords. These can function as VII in the major key or II in the minor key.

EXAMPLE:
Use this F# Locrian mode when soloing over F#m7b5.

NOTE:
Some of you may have noticed that the patterns used for the E Aeolian mode are the same as those used for F# Locrian. The only difference between E Aeolian and F# Locrian is in the note of emphasis. In F# Locrian we want to orient (phrase from) to the F# notes.

LOCRIAN

1

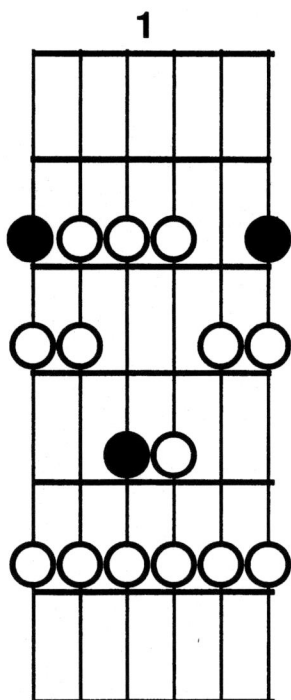

2

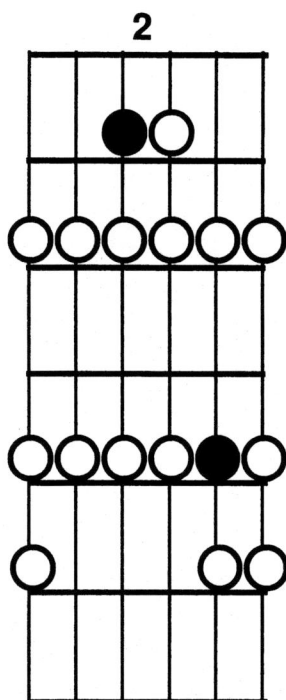

3

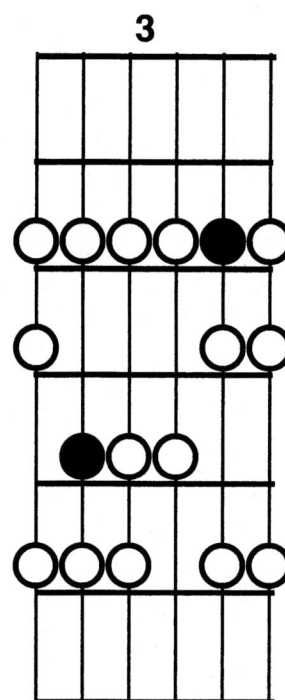

4

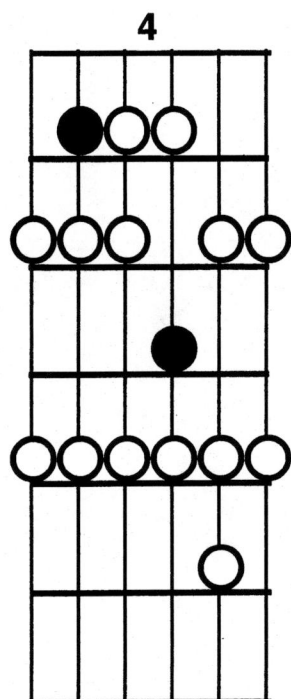

5

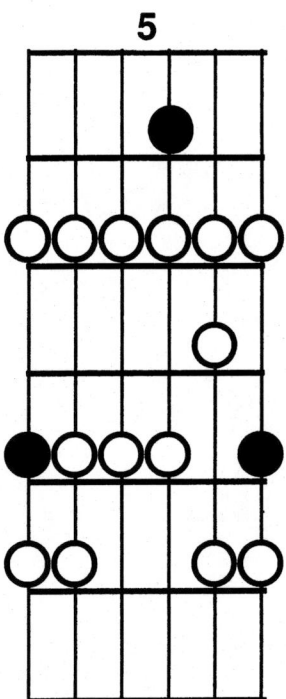

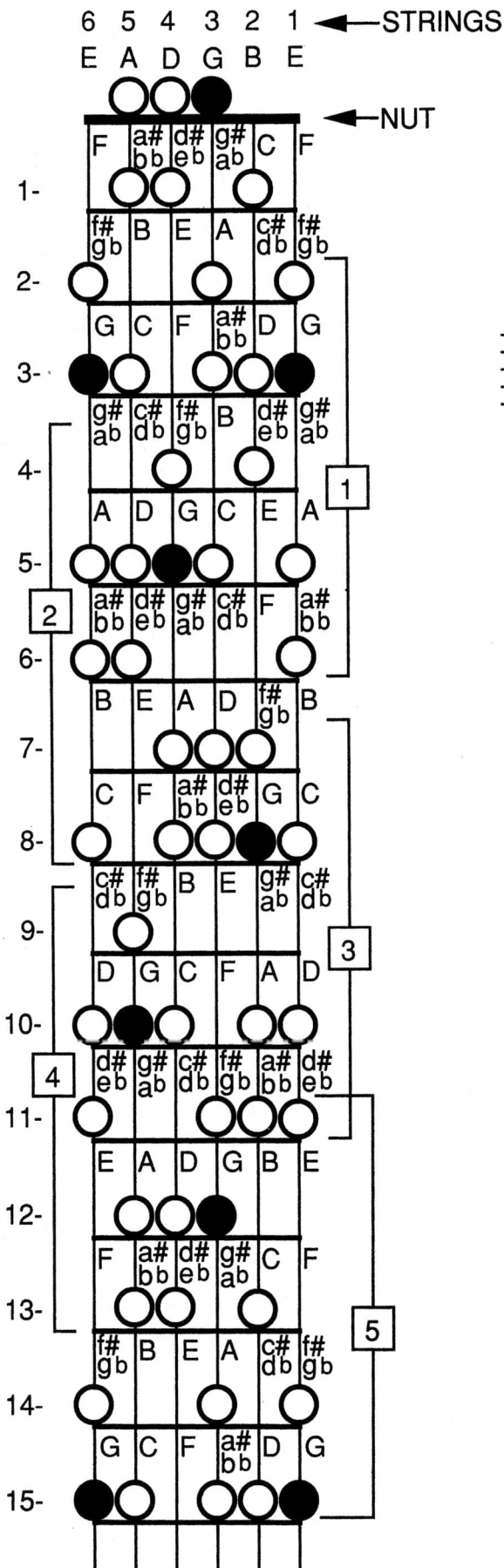

HARMONIC MINOR #1

1-2-b3-4-5-b6-7

ALTERNATE NAMES:
none

PRIMARY USE:
The Harmonic minor is used over minor type chords, such as minor triads, minor add9, and min #7. It does not sound great over min6, min6/9, min7, min9, min13 and min11 because these chords contains pitches which are not in the scale. Despite this statement, it is possible to use this scale anyplace you might normally play the Aeolian scale.

EXAMPLE:
Use the G harmonic minor for soloing over any of the above mentioned chords as long as their respective roots are all G notes.

HARMONIC MINOR #1

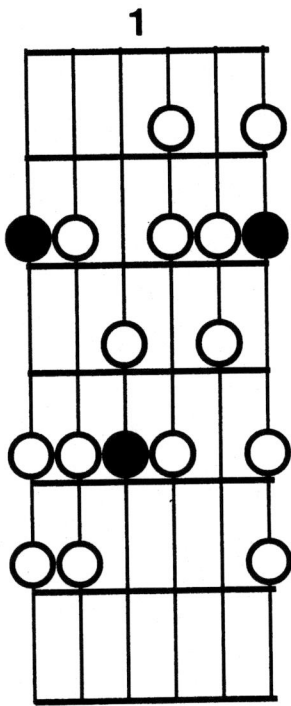

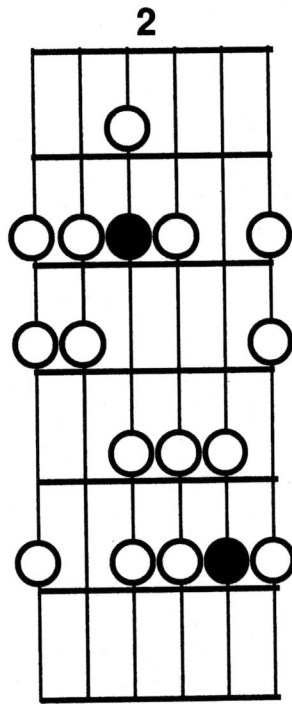

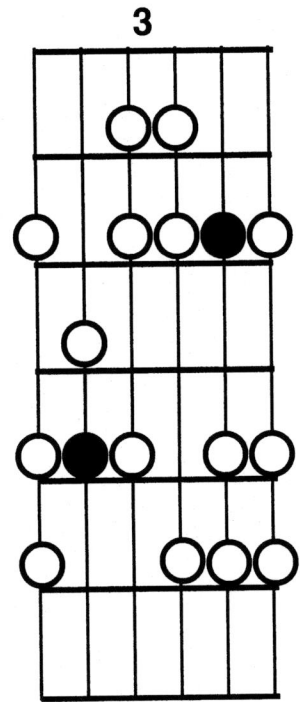

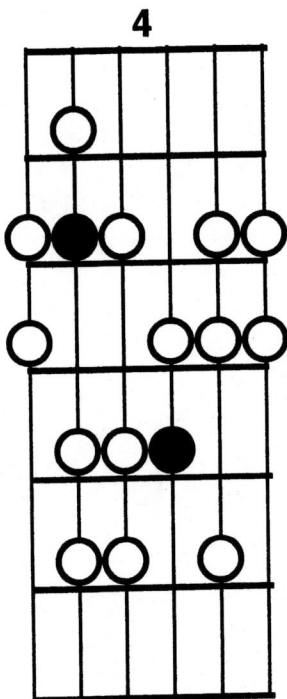

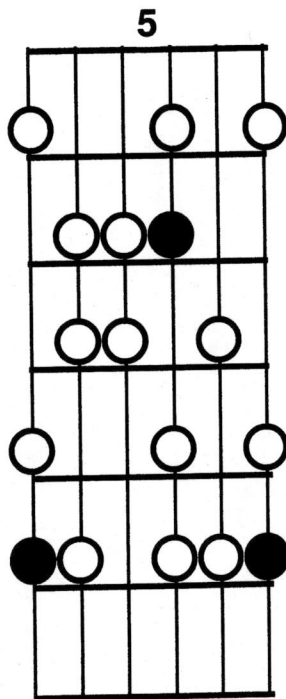

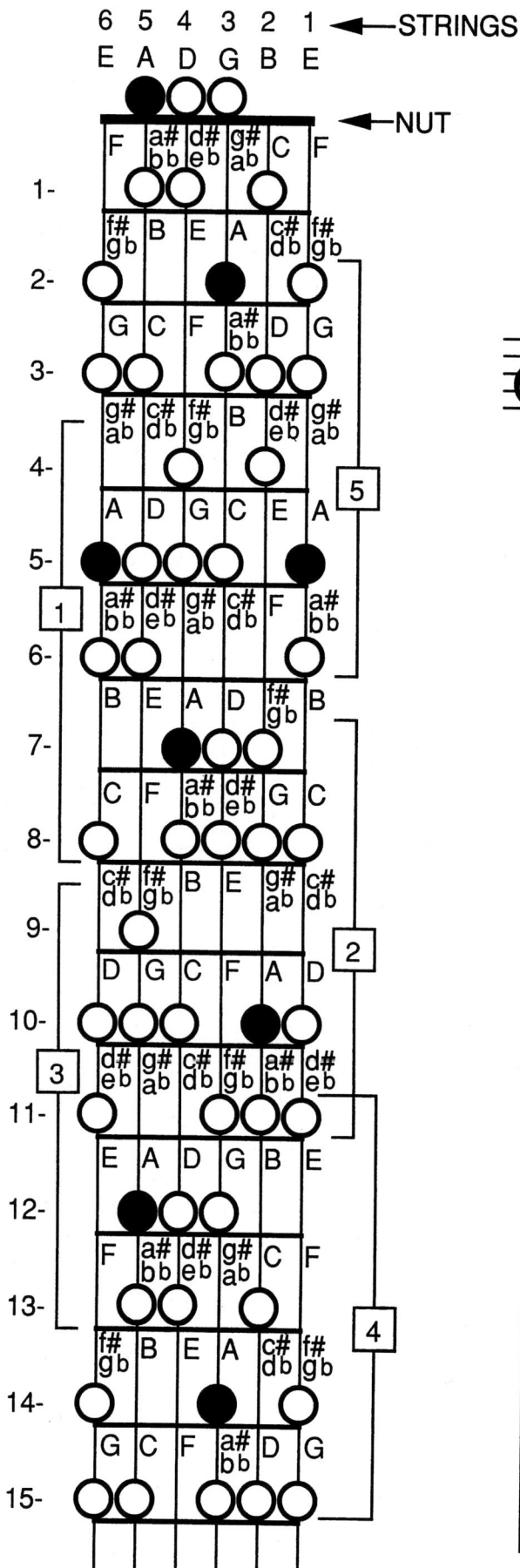

HARMONIC MINOR #2

1-b2-b3-4-b5-6-b7

ALTERNATE NAMES:
none

PRIMARY USE:
The Harmonic minor #2 is used over min7b5 chords. These chords are also called half-diminished.

EXAMPLE:
Use the A harmonic minor #2 for soloing over an Am7b5 chord.

HARMONIC MINOR #2

28

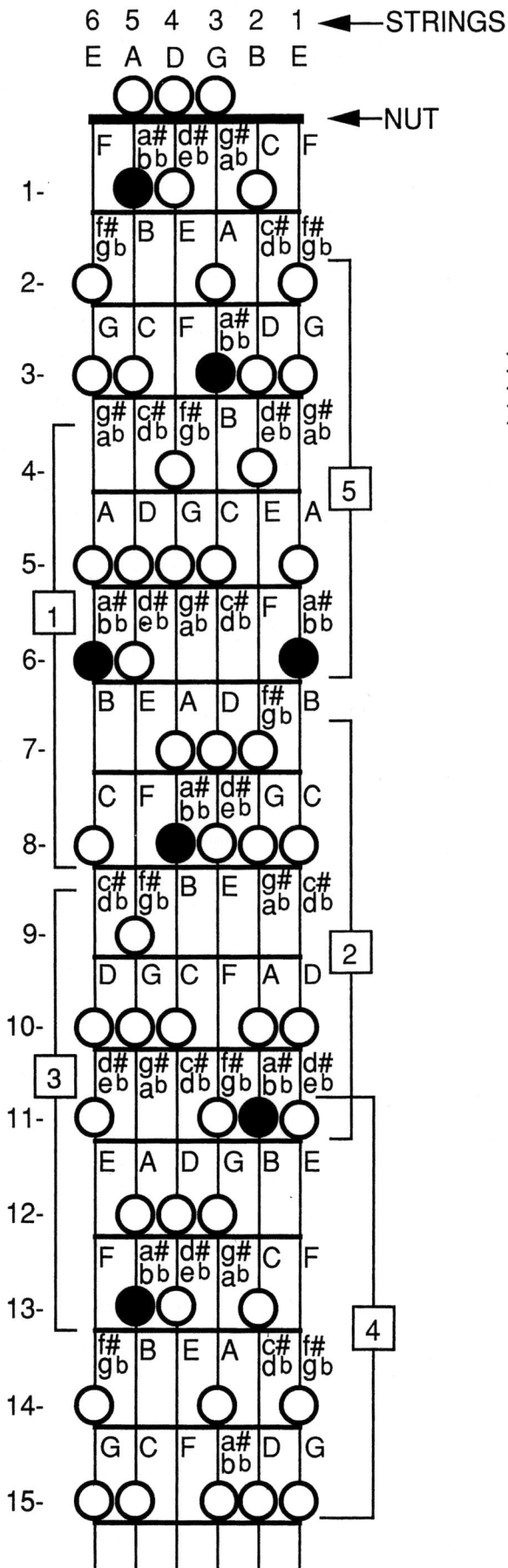

HARMONIC MINOR #3

1-2-3-4-#5-6-7

ALTERNATE NAMES:
none

PRIMARY USE:
The Harmonic minor #3 is used over major 7th chords which contain a raised 5th. Although this is a rare chord, it is used from time to time by contemporary jazz writers.

EXAMPLE:
Use the Bb harmonic minor #3 for soloing over Bbmaj7#5.

HARMONIC MINOR #3

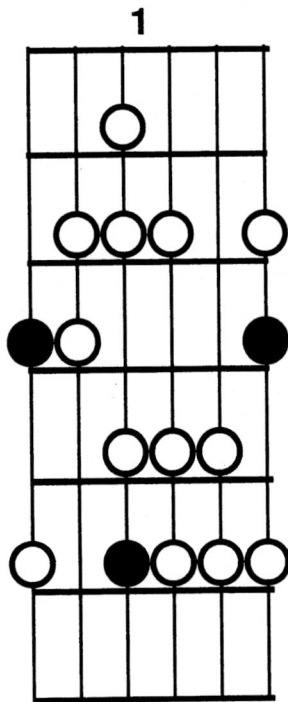

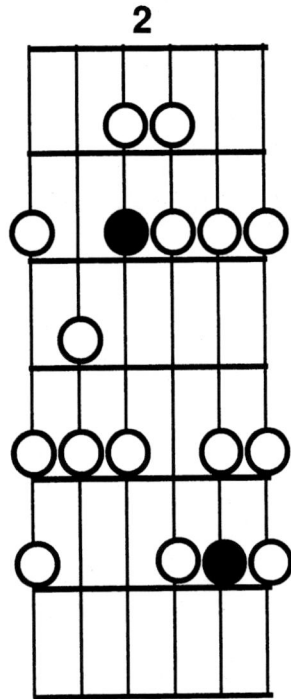

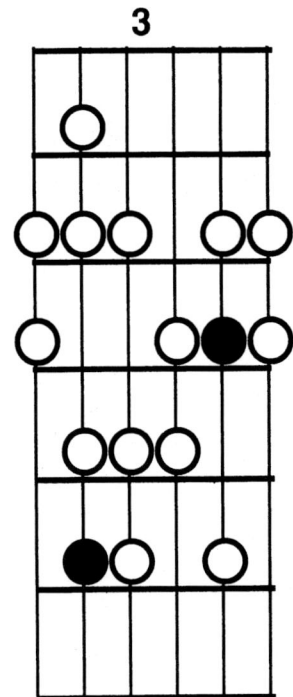

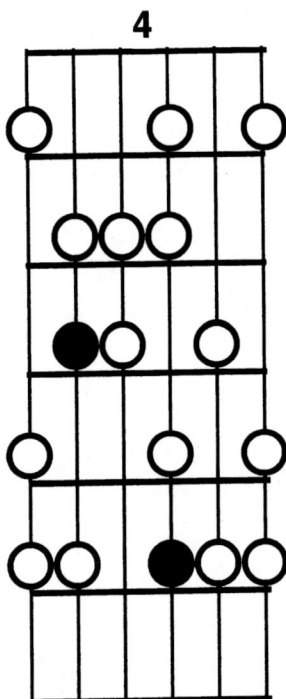

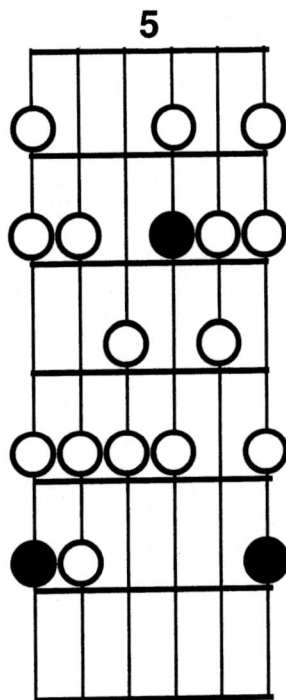

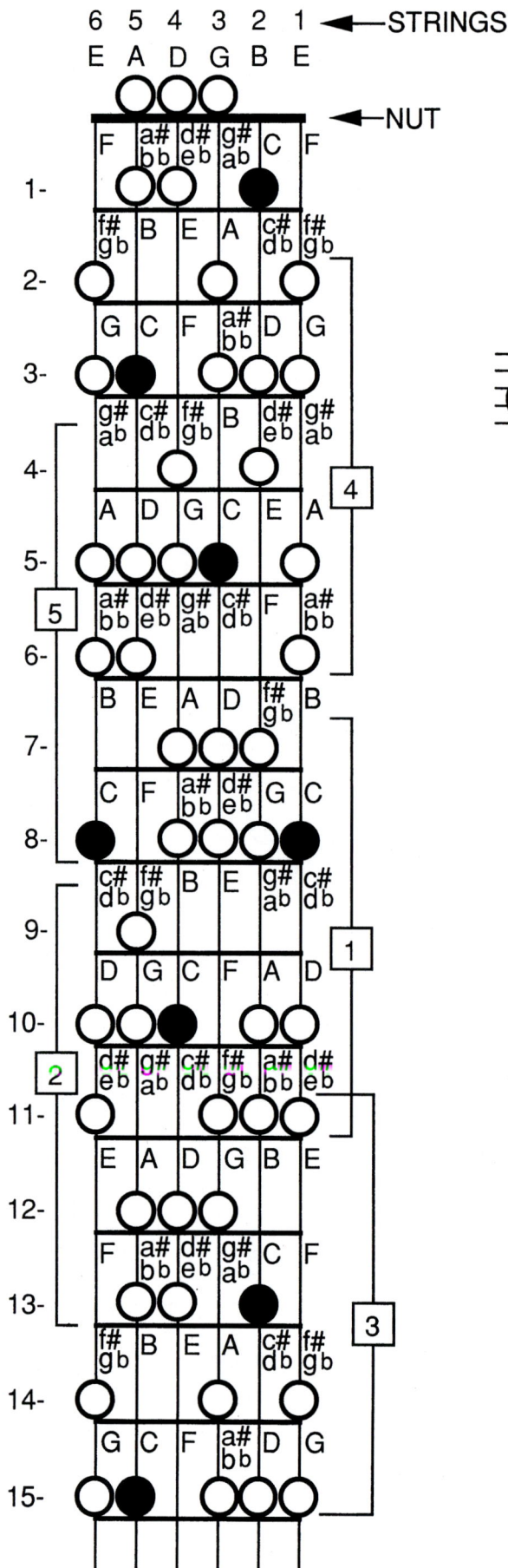

HARMONIC MINOR #4

1-2-b3-#4-5-6-b7

ALTERNATE NAMES:
none

PRIMARY USE:
The Harmonic minor #4 is used over minor triads, minor 7th chords with a flatted 5th, (also known as min7b5 chords). Because this scale is so similar to the Blues scale (see Blues scale type B) you could use it over dominant 7th chords, especially those with either a #9, b5 or #11.

EXAMPLE:
Use the C harmonic minor #4 for soloing over Cm7, Cm7b5, C7, C7#9, C7b5 and C7#11.

HARMONIC MINOR #4

1

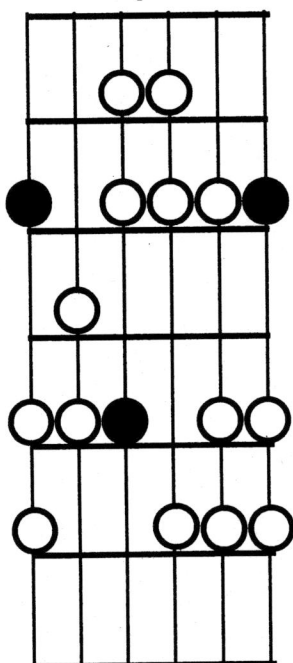

2

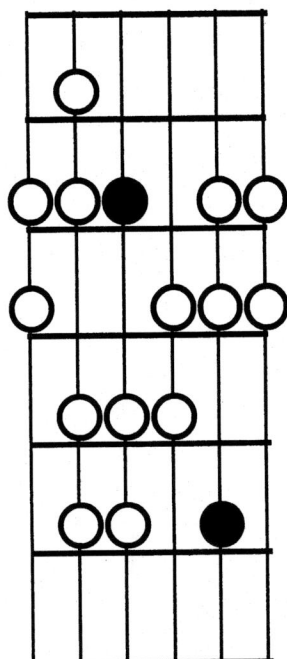

3

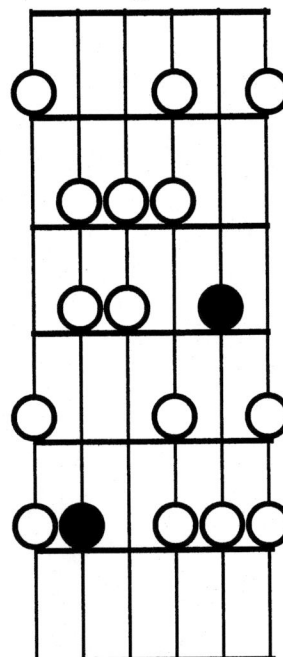

4

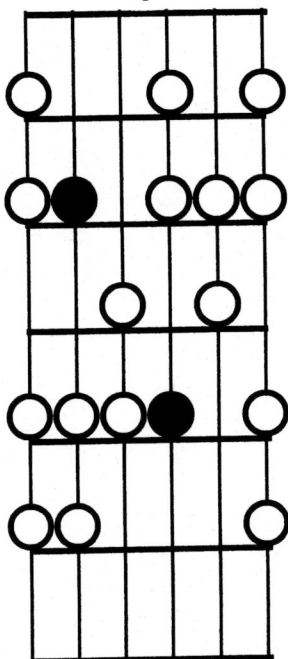

5

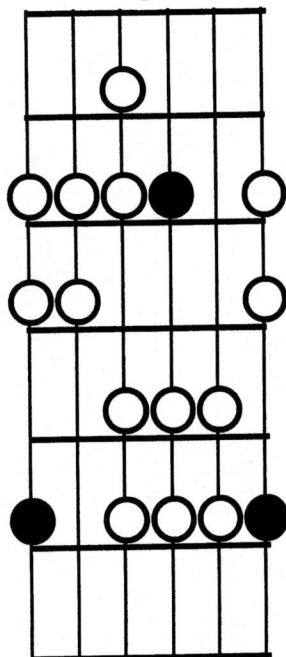

32

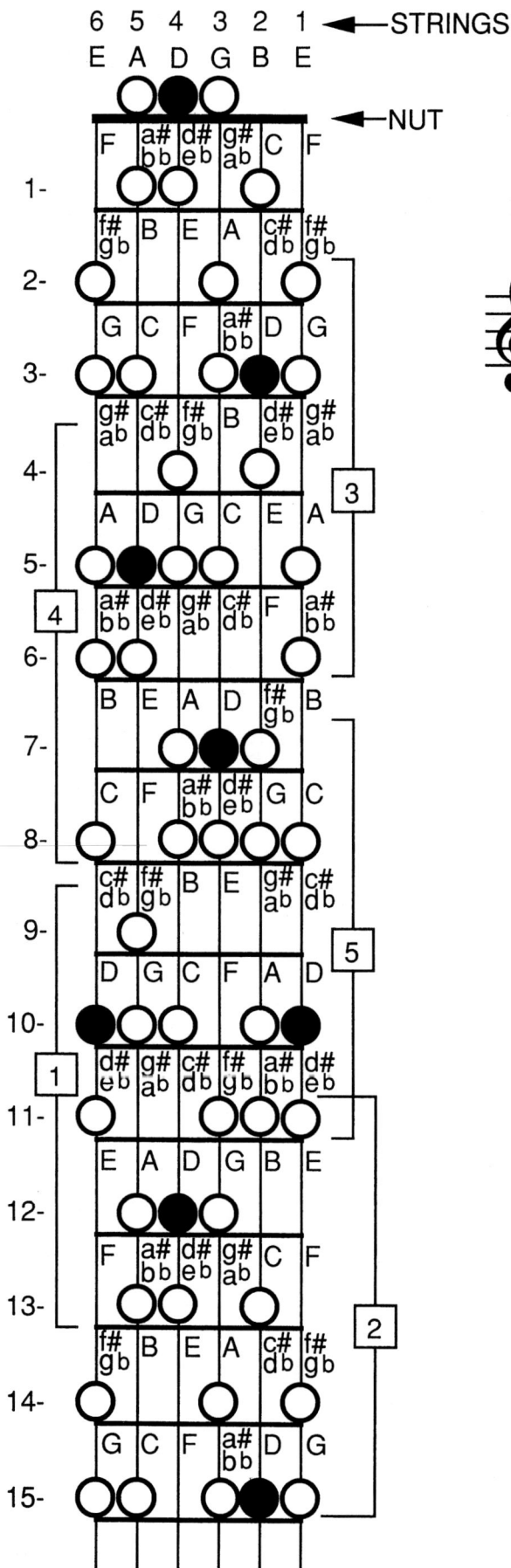

HARMONIC MINOR #5

1-b2-3-4-5-b6-b7

ALTERNATE NAMES:
none

PRIMARY USE:
The Harmonic minor #5 is used over dominant type chords which have either a raised 5th and/or a flatted 9th. These chords are often given the name "altered". You could also use this scale over unaltered dominant chords such as dom7, dom9 and dom13. You'd be superimposing an altered sound over an unaltered chord. To some, this might sound like a mistake, but it is a common practice in jazz improvisation.

EXAMPLE:
Use the D harmonic minor #5 for soloing over D7, D9, D13, D7b5, D9b5, D7b9, D7#9 or any D dominant which has a #5 or b9 (or both).

HARMONIC MINOR #5

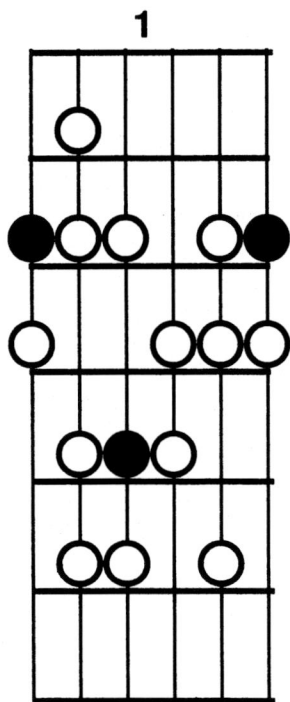

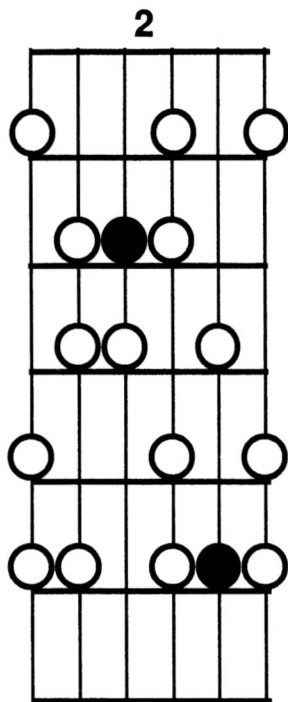

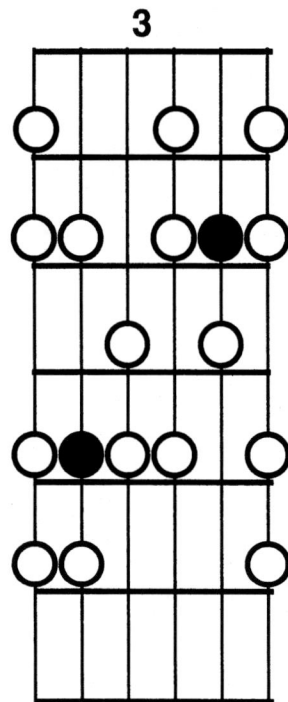

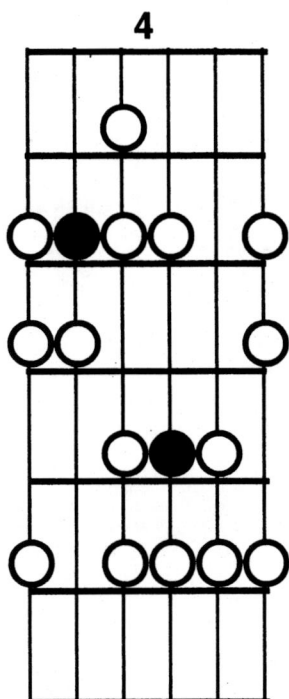

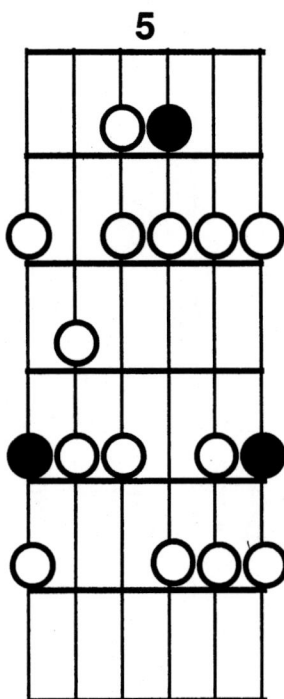

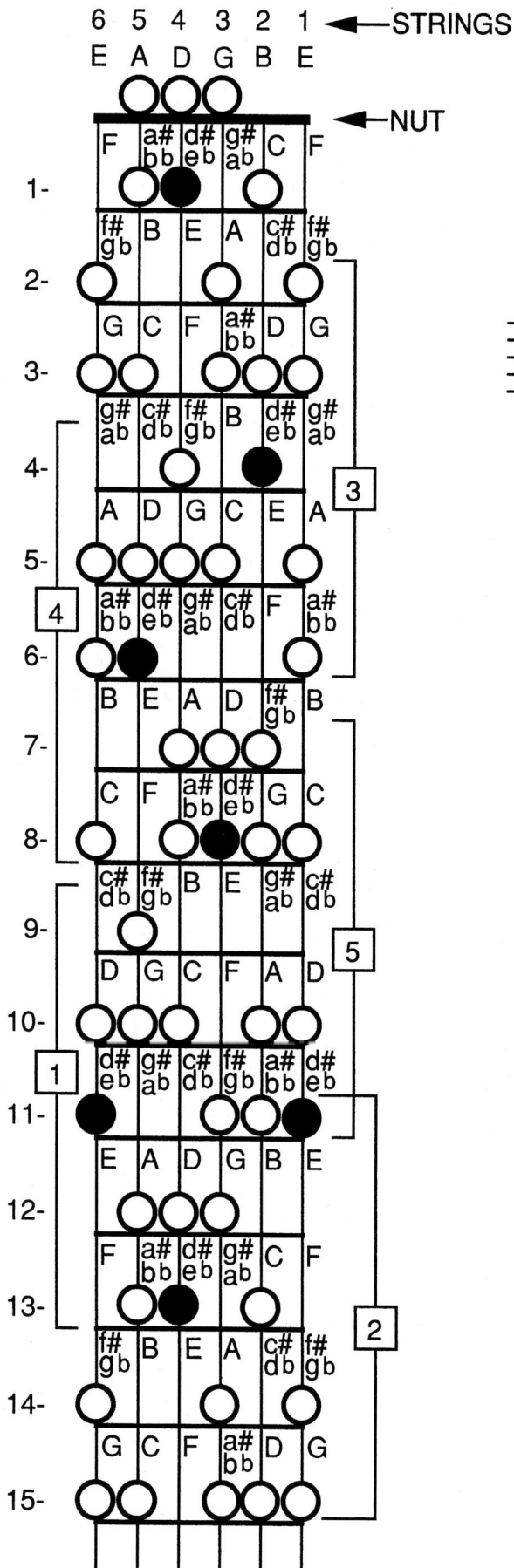

HARMONIC MINOR #6

1-#2-♮3-#4-5-6-7

ALTERNATE NAMES:
none

PRIMARY USE:
The Harmonic minor #6 is an unusual scale. It has a major 3rd and 7th interval as well as a lowered 3rd. The lowered 3rd can be thought of as a #9 too. However, there aren't many major 7th chords which also contain a #9. This scale could be used over a major7#11 chord for a blues sound (caused by the b3).

EXAMPLE:
Use the Eb harmonic minor #6 for soloing over Eb, Ebmaj7#4, Ebmaj7b5 and Ebmaj7#11.

HARMONIC MINOR #6

1

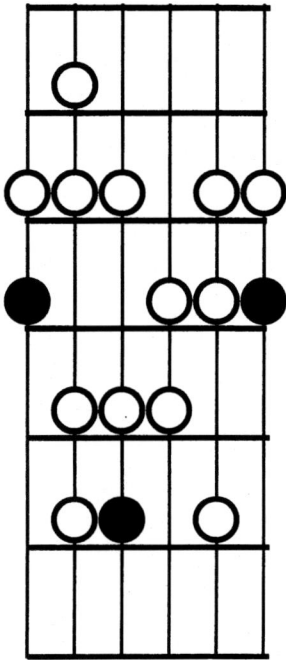

2

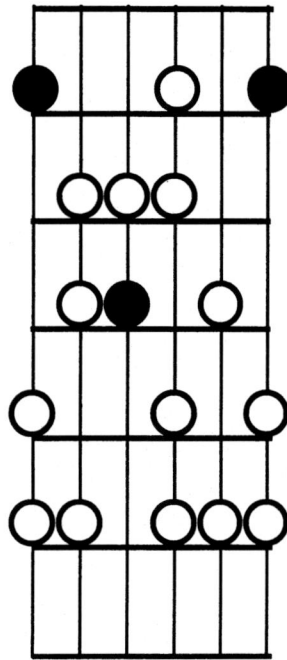

3

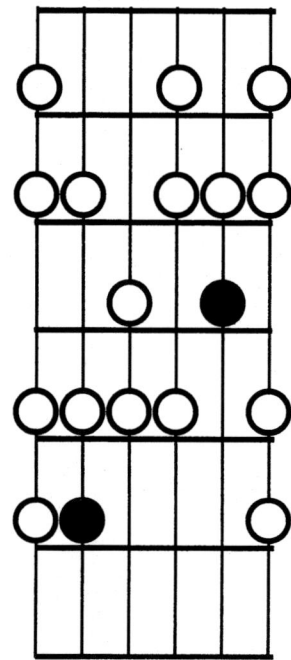

4

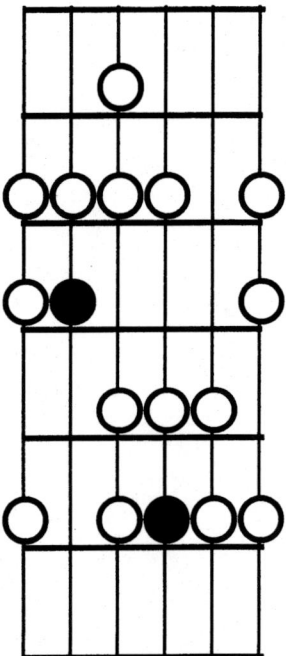

5

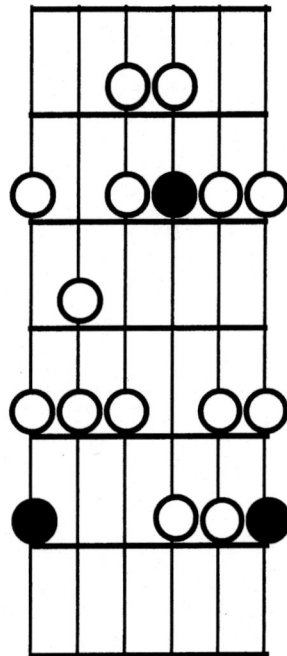

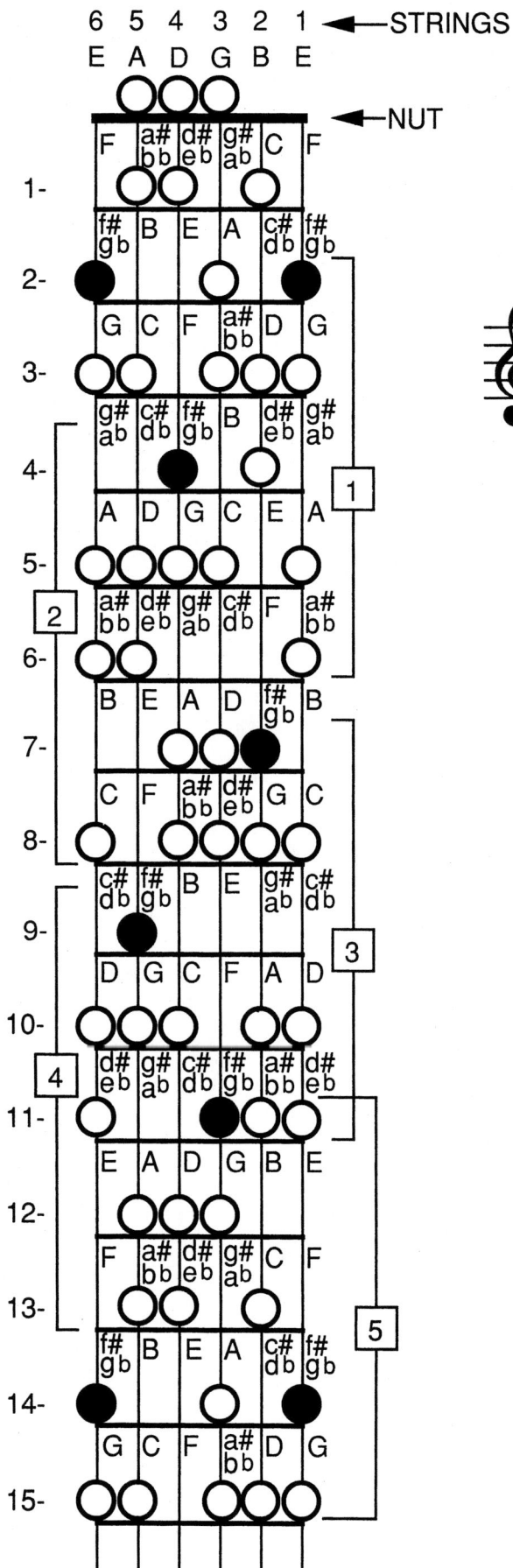

HARMONIC MINOR #7

1-b2-b3-b4-b5-b6-bb7

ALTERNATE NAMES:
none

PRIMARY USE:
The Harmonic minor #7 is used over diminished triads and diminished 7th chords.

EXAMPLE:
Use the F# harmonic minor #7 for soloing over F#dim and F#dim7.

HARMONIC MINOR #7

1

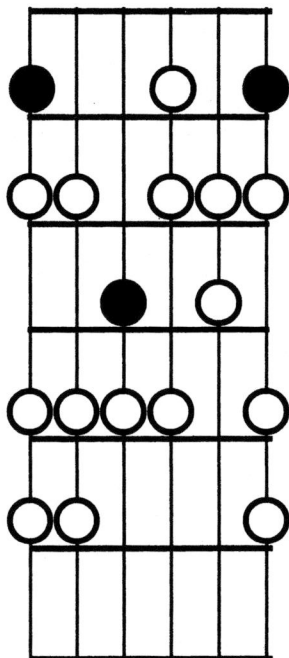

2

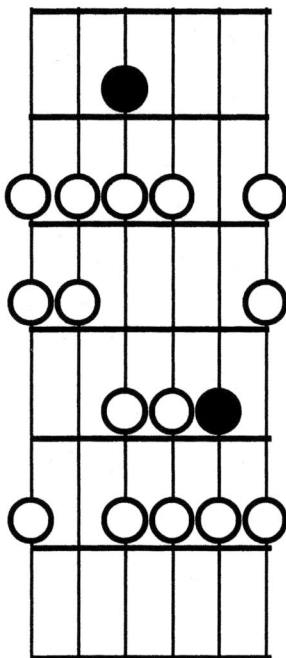

3

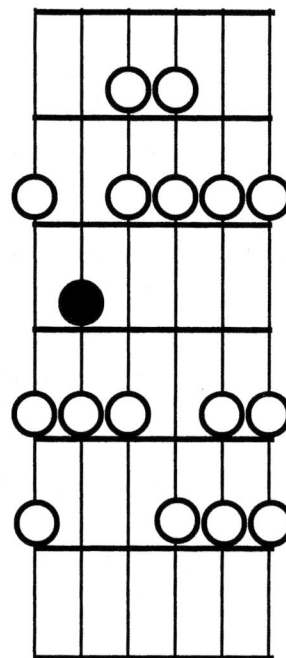

4

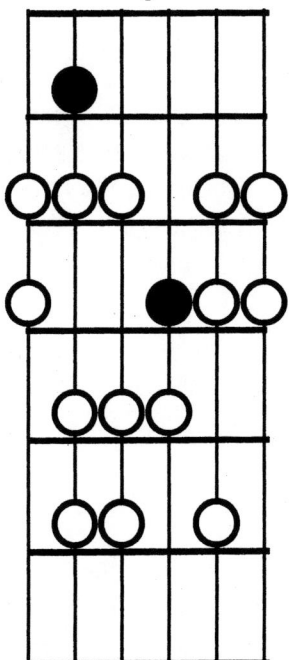

5

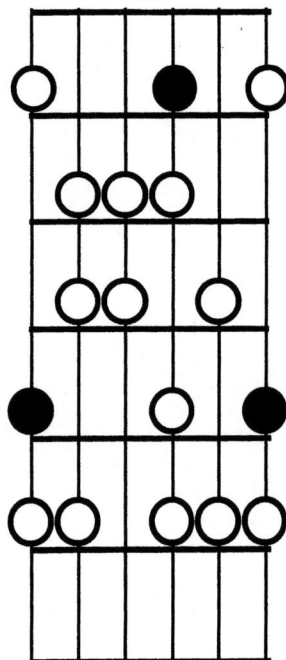

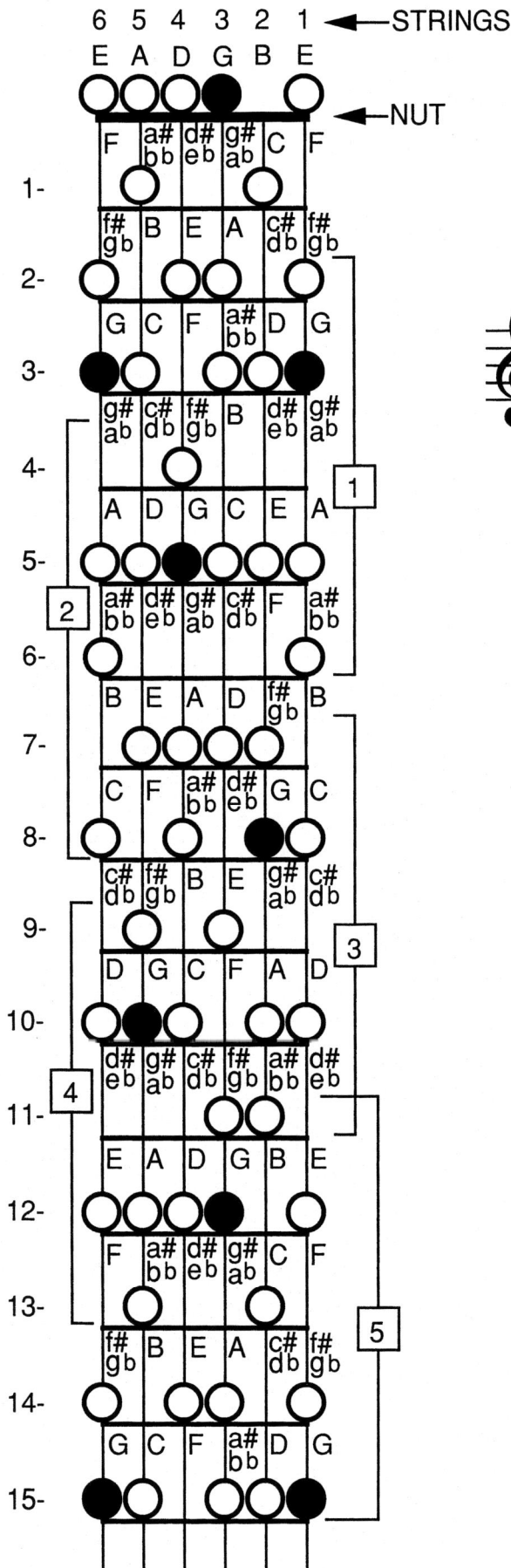

MELODIC MINOR #1

1-2-b3-4-5-6-7

ALTERNATE NAMES:

The ascending melodic minor is often called the Jazz Minor to differentiate it from the melodic minor scale used in Classical music. Classical theory recognizes an ascending and a descending version of the melodic minor scale. On the way up, the formula is 1-2-b3-4-5-6-7 and on the way down, it's 1-2-b3-4-5-b6-b7, or what we call the natural minor scale (Aeolian mode). Jazz players just use the ascending melodic minor for improvising.

PRIMARY USE:

The Melodic or Jazz Minor is used to solo over minor type chords such as min triads, min6, min6/9, min11, min9, min add9 and min#7 chords. Try using this scale anytime you might use the Aeolian mode.

EXAMPLE:

Use the G Melodic Minor for soloing over any of the above mentioned chords as long as their respective roots are all G notes.

MELODIC MIN.#1

1

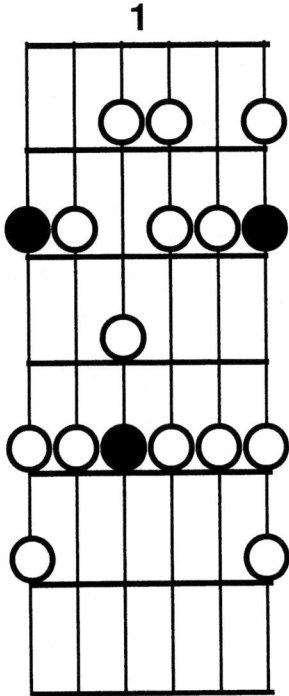

2

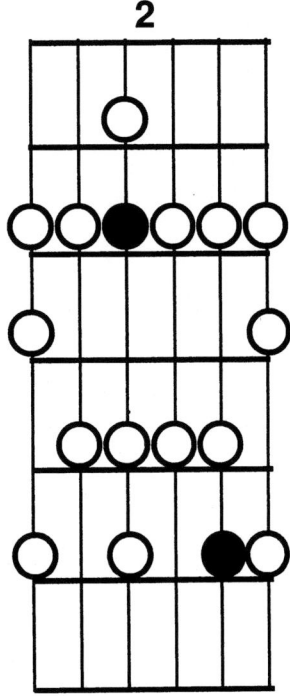

3

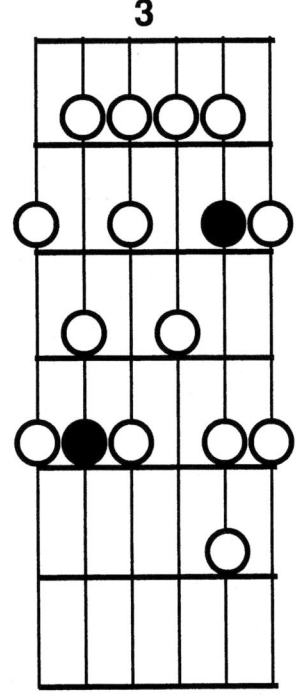

4

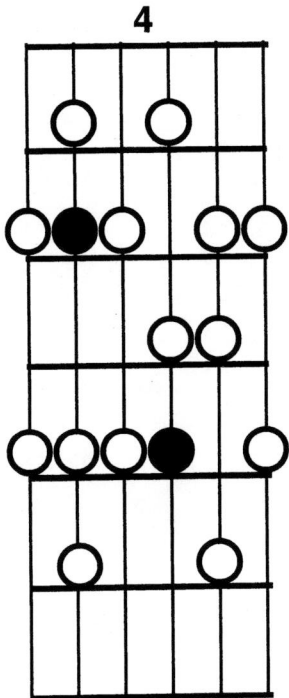

5

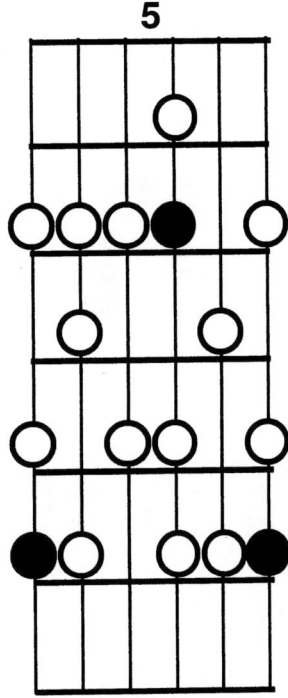

40

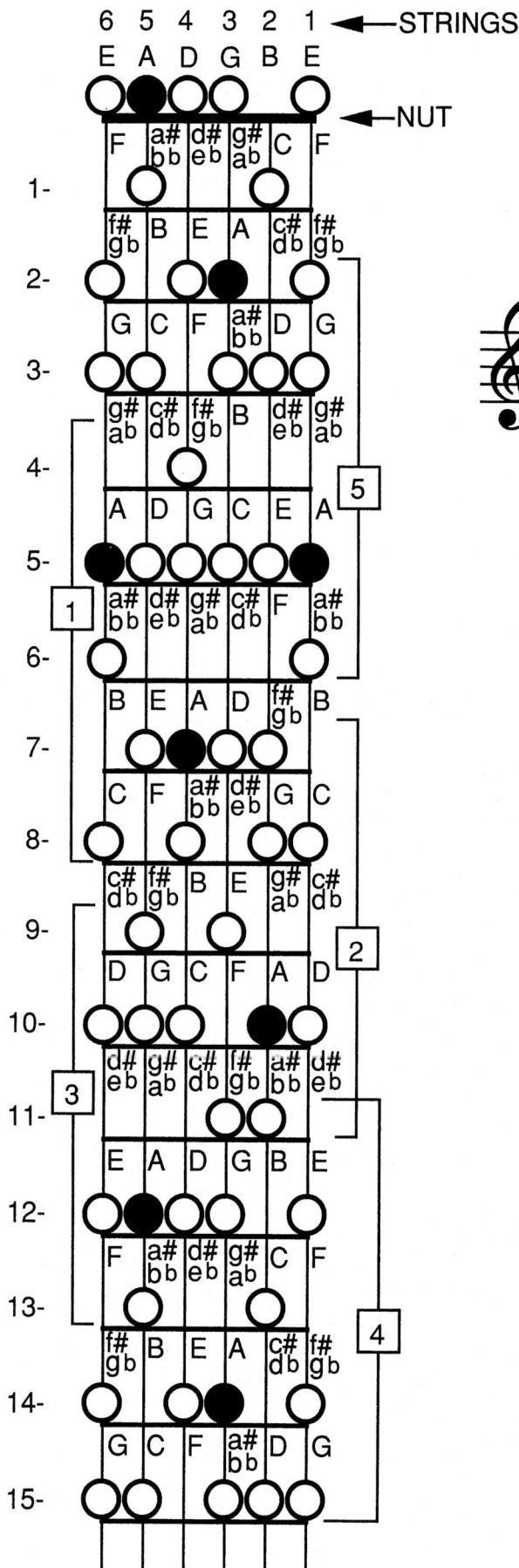

MELODIC MINOR #2

1-b2-b3-4-5-6-b7

ALTERNATE NAMES:
The second mode of the melodic minor scale is often called the Dorian b2 scale because it is just that. It has the same formula as the Dorian mode with the exception of the lowered 2nd degree.

PRIMARY USE:
Although not one of the most popular modes of melodic minor, it still can be used over minor type chords such as a min. triad, min6, min6/9, min7, min11, etc. It is especially appropriate if the min. chord has a flatted 9th.

EXAMPLE:
Use the A melodic minor #2 over any of the above chords, making sure that A is the root note of each chord.

MELODIC MIN.#2

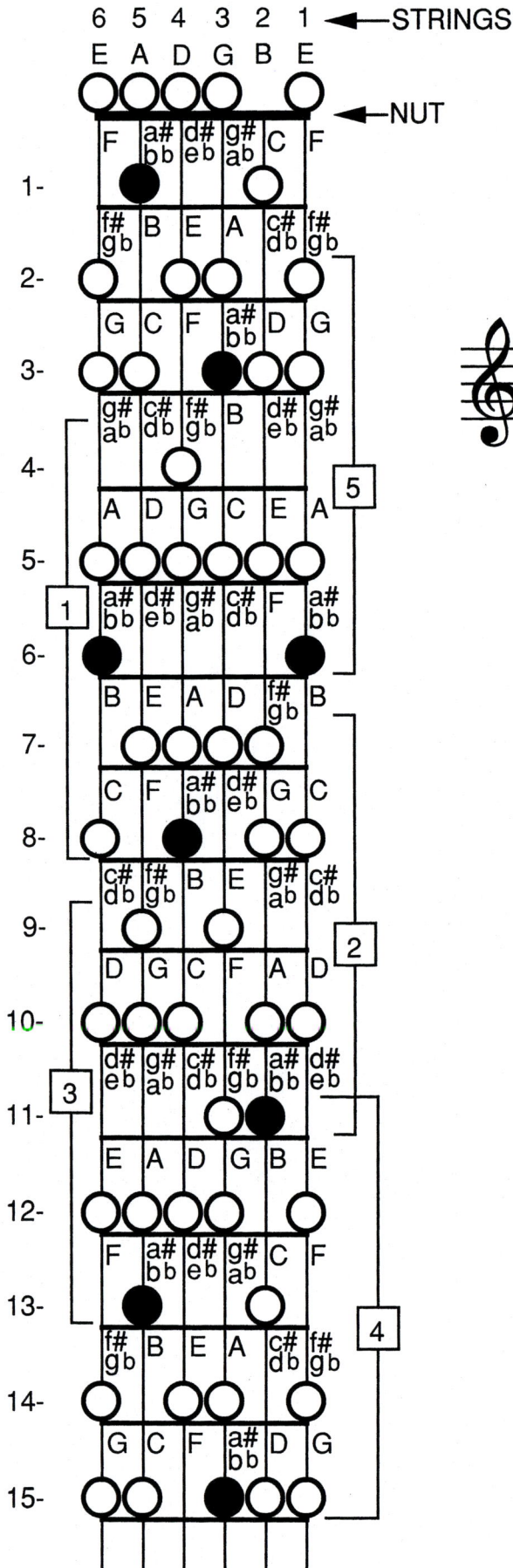

MELODIC MINOR #3

1-2-3-#4-#5-6-7

ALTERNATE NAMES:
The 3rd mode of the Melodic minor scale is also known as the Lydian-Augmented scale. Lydian refers to the #4 in the scale and Augmented refers to the #5.

PRIMARY USE:
Although not one of the most popular modes of melodic minor, it still can be used over major chords which contain either a #4, b5, #11 or #5. Use it over such chords as: maj7b5, maj7#4, maj7#11 or maj7#5. The #5 will be the pitch that will raise eyebrows simply because we don't often hear this alteration to the major sound.

EXAMPLE:
Use the Bb Lydian-Augmented scale over any of the above chords, making sure that Bb is the root note of each chord.

MELODIC MIN.#3

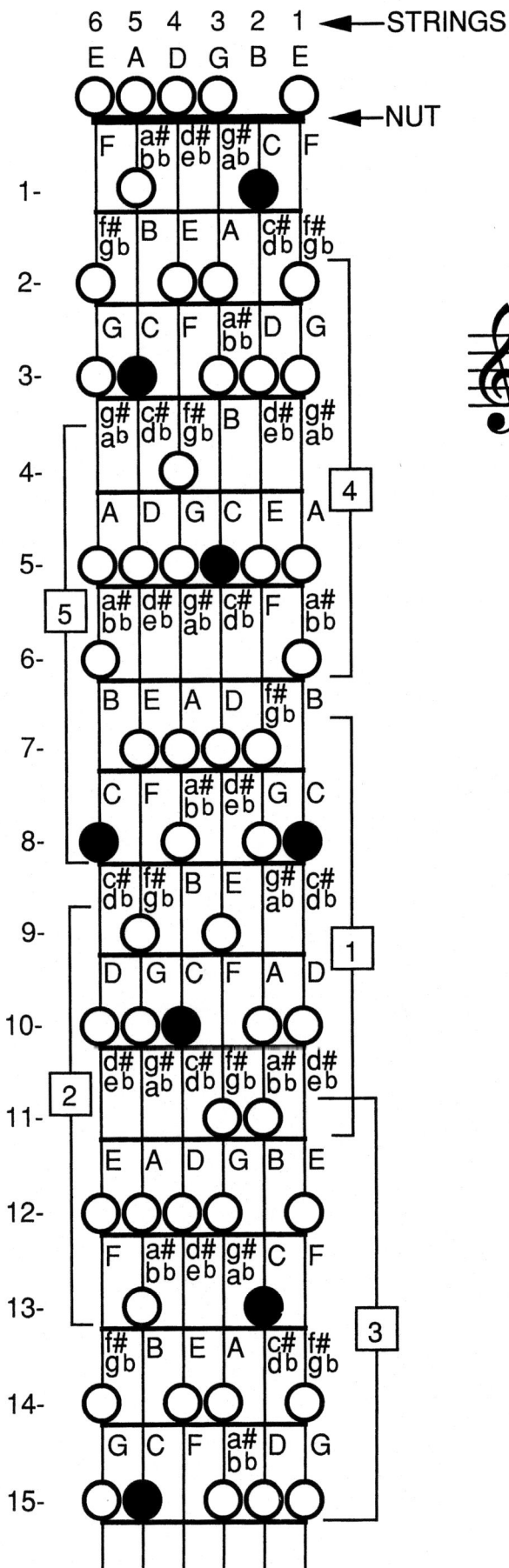

MELODIC MINOR #4

1-2-3-#4-5-6-b7

STRINGS — 6 5 4 3 2 1 — E A D G B E

ALTERNATE NAMES:
The 4th mode of the Melodic Minor is also called Lydian Dominant or Lydian b7. This is because it contains a raised 4th, thus the origin of Lydian. The lowered 7th is where the dominant comes from.

PRIMARY USE:
This is a popular mode with Jazz players because it works so well over dominant chords. The #4 and b7 give this mode a bluesy sound. Use it over dom7, dom9, dom13, dom7b5, dom7#11, dom7#4 or over any dom7 type chord which has a lowered 5th, raised 4th or raised 11th.

EXAMPLE:
Use the C Lydian-Dominant scale over any of the above chords, making sure that C is the root note of each chord.

MELODIC MIN.#4

1

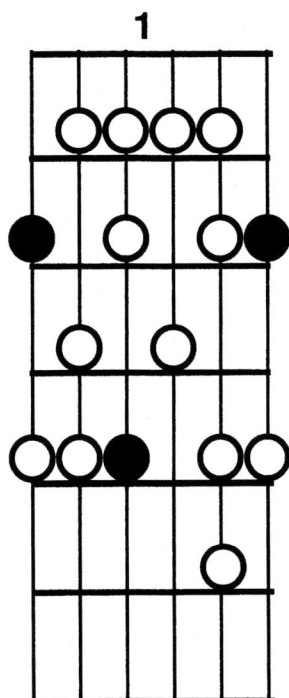

2

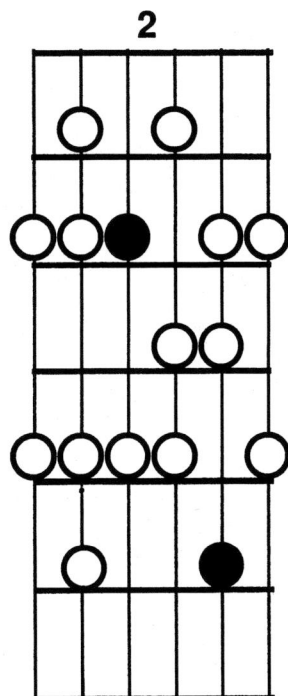

3

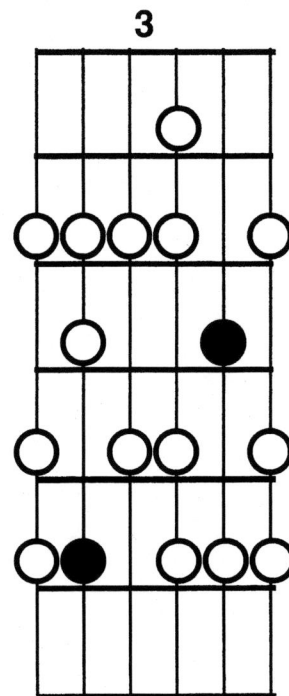

4

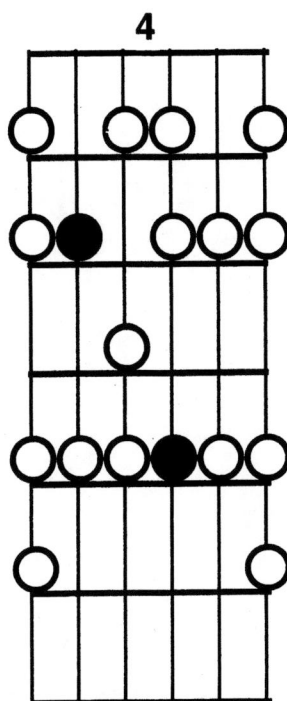

5

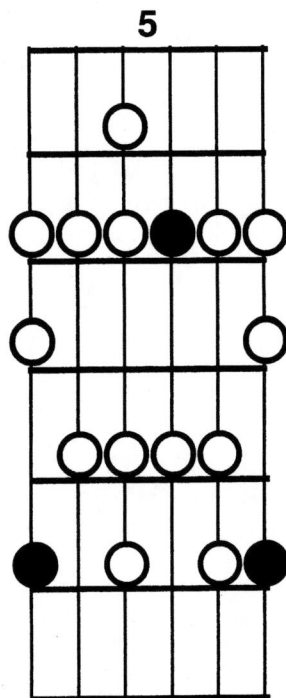

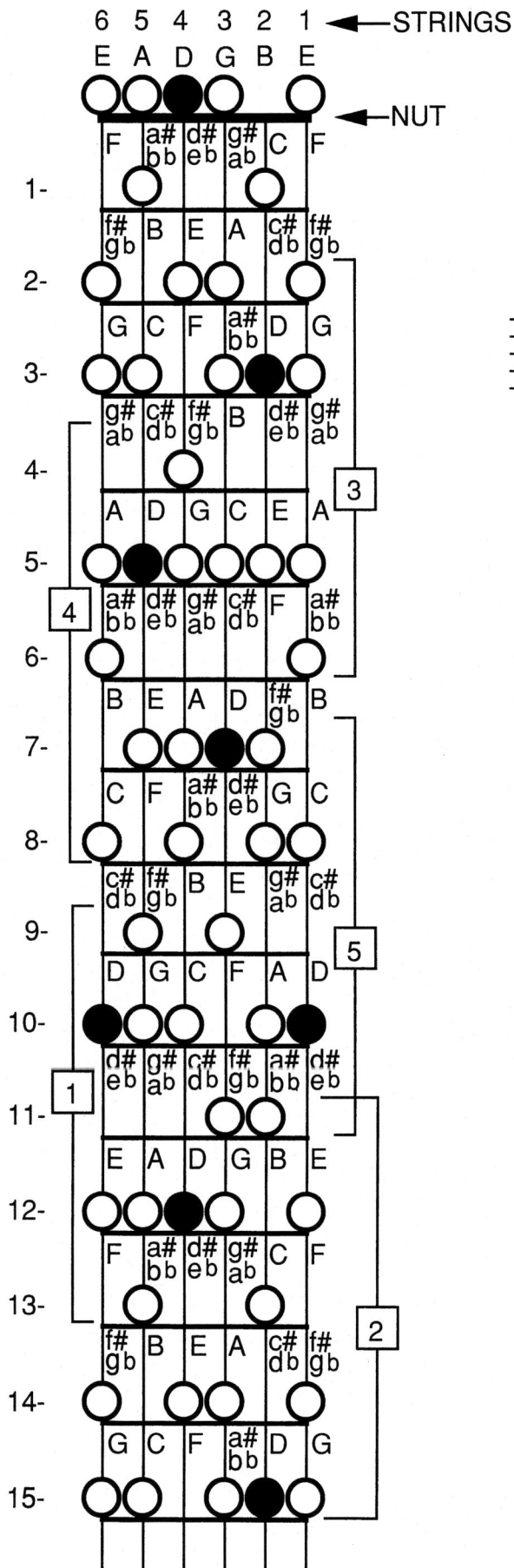

MELODIC MINOR #5

1-2-3-4-5-b6-b7

ALTERNATE NAMES:
The 5th mode of the Melodic Minor is also called Mixolydian b6. This is because it is just like the Mixolydian mode with the addition of a lowered 6th degree.

PRIMARY USE:
This mode can be used over dom7 type chords which contain a #5 (this is the musical equivalent of a b6). You could also use it over any dom7 type which contains a b6 or b13, although these chords are very rare. As such, this mode isn't used much.

EXAMPLE:
Use the D Mixolydian b6 scale over any of the above chords, making sure that D is the root note of each chord.

MELODIC MIN.#5

1

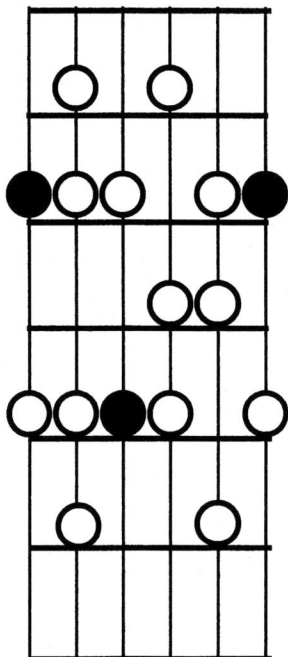

2

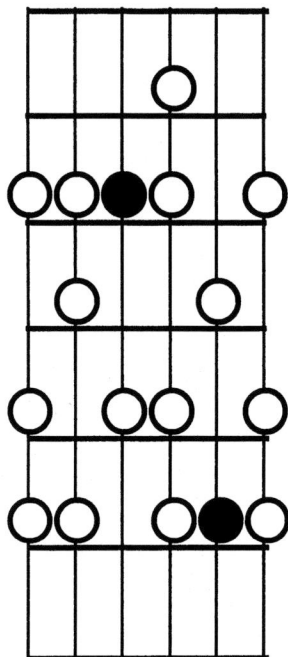

3

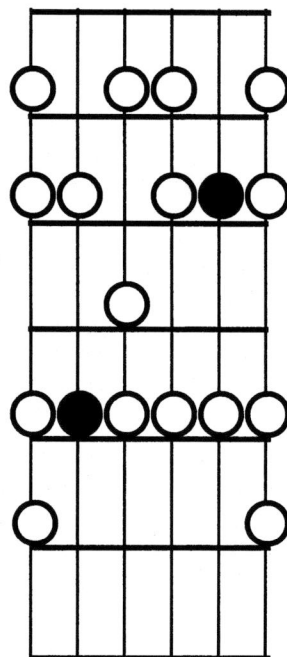

4

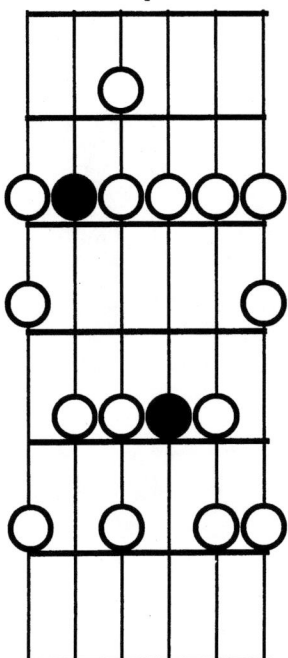

5

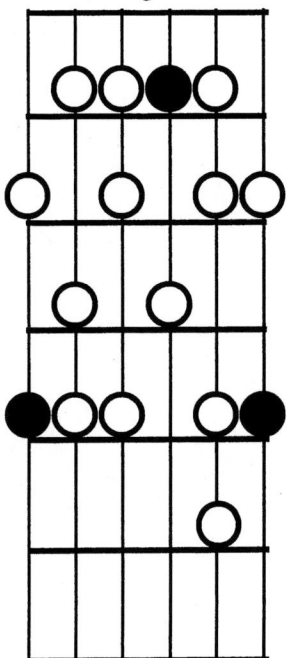

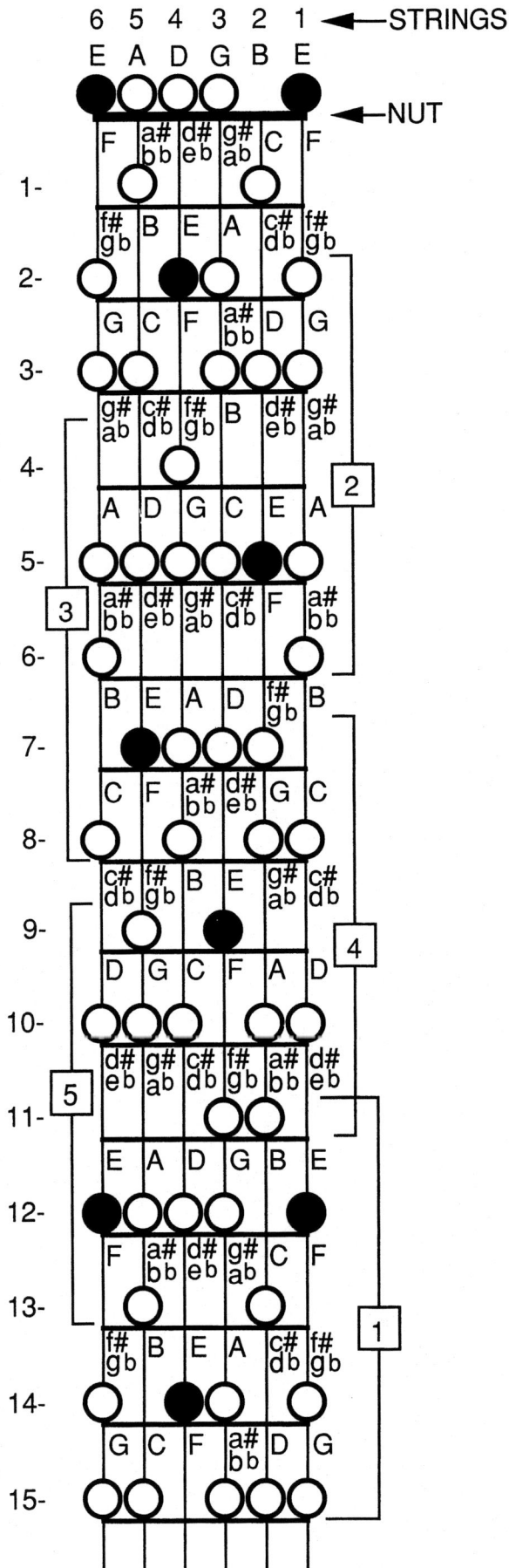

MELODIC MINOR #6

1-2-b3-4-b5-b6-b7

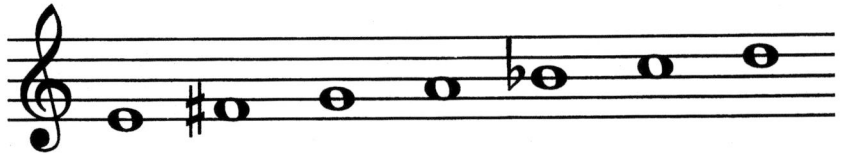

ALTERNATE NAMES:
The 6th mode of the Melodic Minor is also called the Locrian #2 scale (the #2 is the equivalent in sound to the b3).

PRIMARY USE:
This mode can be used over the half-diminished chord, also known as a min7b5.

EXAMPLE:
Use the E Locrian #2 scale over Em7b5.

MELODIC MIN.#6

1

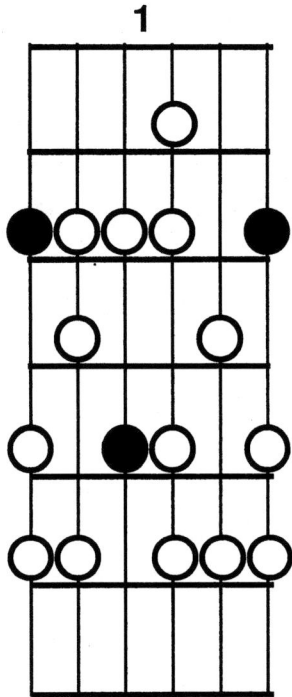

2

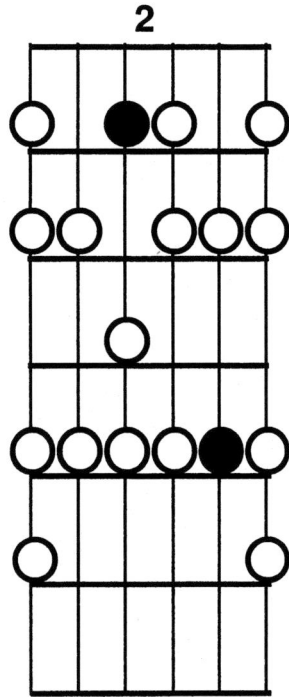

3

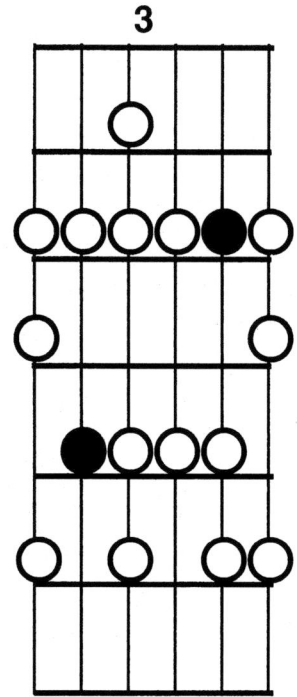

4

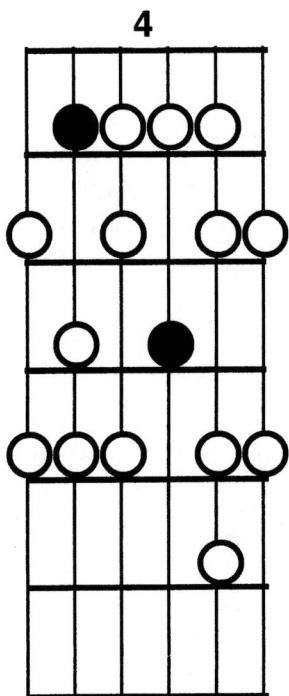

5

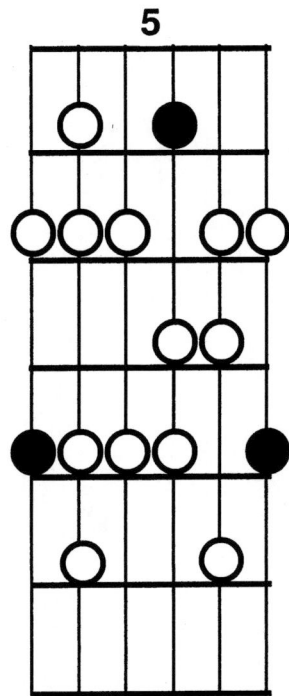

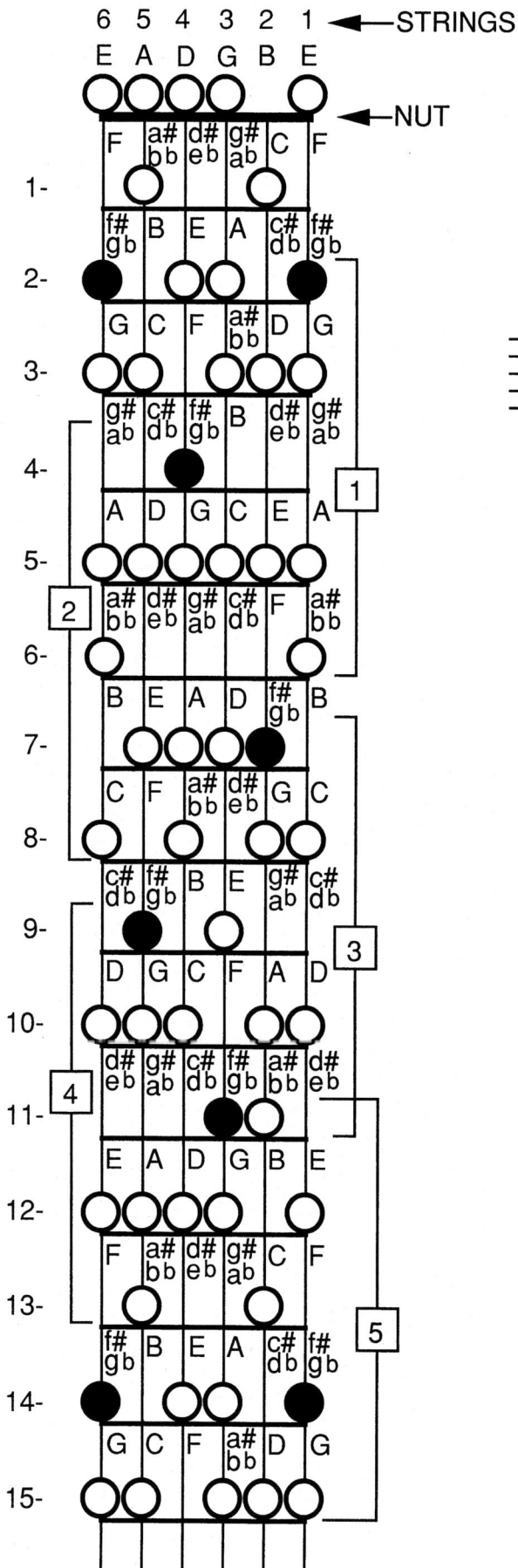

MELODIC MINOR #7

1-b2-b3-b4-b5-b6-b7

ALTERNATE NAMES:

The 7th mode of the Melodic Minor is also called the Super Locrian scale or the Altered scale. Altered is a good name for this scale because it contains all of the possible alterations to a dominant type chord, the b5, #5 (same as b6), the b9 (same as the b2), and the #9 (same as the b3). It is a very popular mode with Jazz musicians who like to "get outside".

PRIMARY USE:

Use this scale over any dominant chord which contains any of the following alterations: #5, b5, #4, #11, #9, b9 or any combination of these. It's a dissonant sounding mode, so use it when you want tension.

EXAMPLE:

Use the F# Altered scale over any of these: F#7b5, F#7#5, F#7b9, F#7#9, F#7alt., F#7b5b9, F#7b5#9, F#7#5b9 or F#7#5#9.

NOTES:

The first four notes of this scale could be seen as part of a diminished scale (H/W) and the rest of the scale as forming a whole-tone scale. (See these scale patterns for clarification.)

MELODIC MIN.#7

1

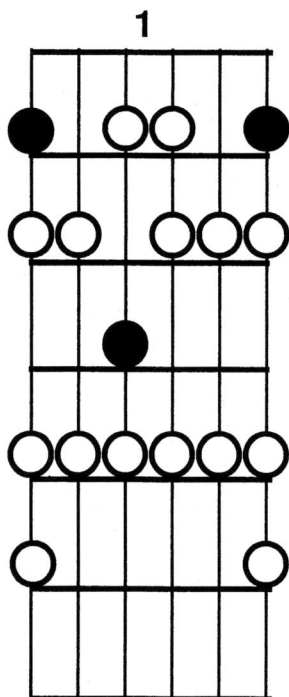

2

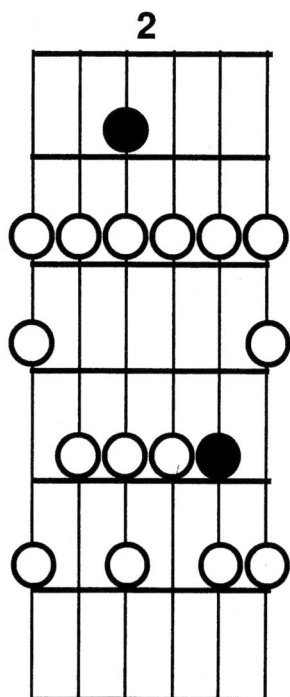

3

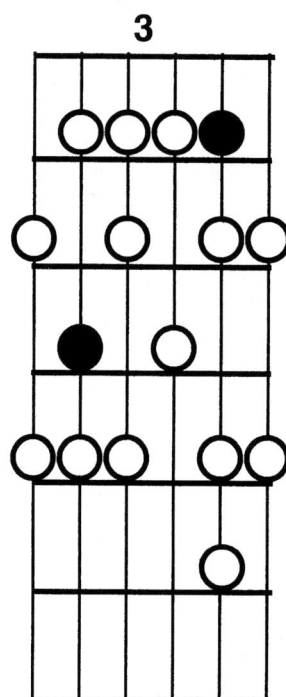

4

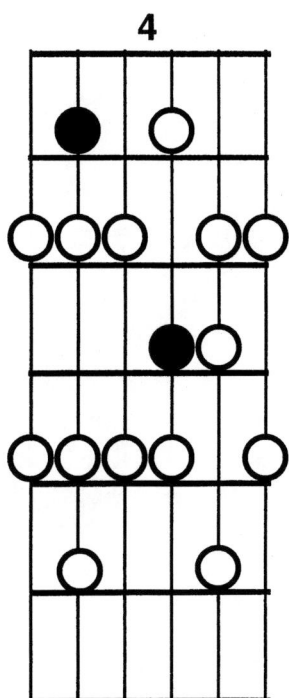

5

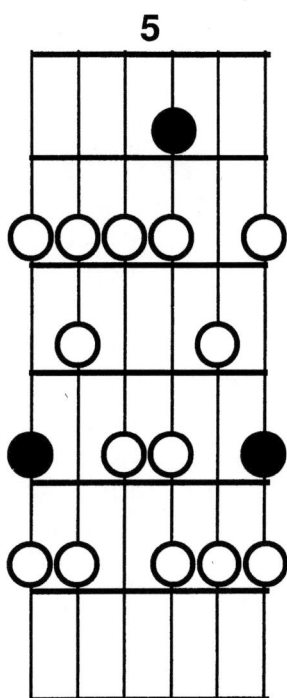

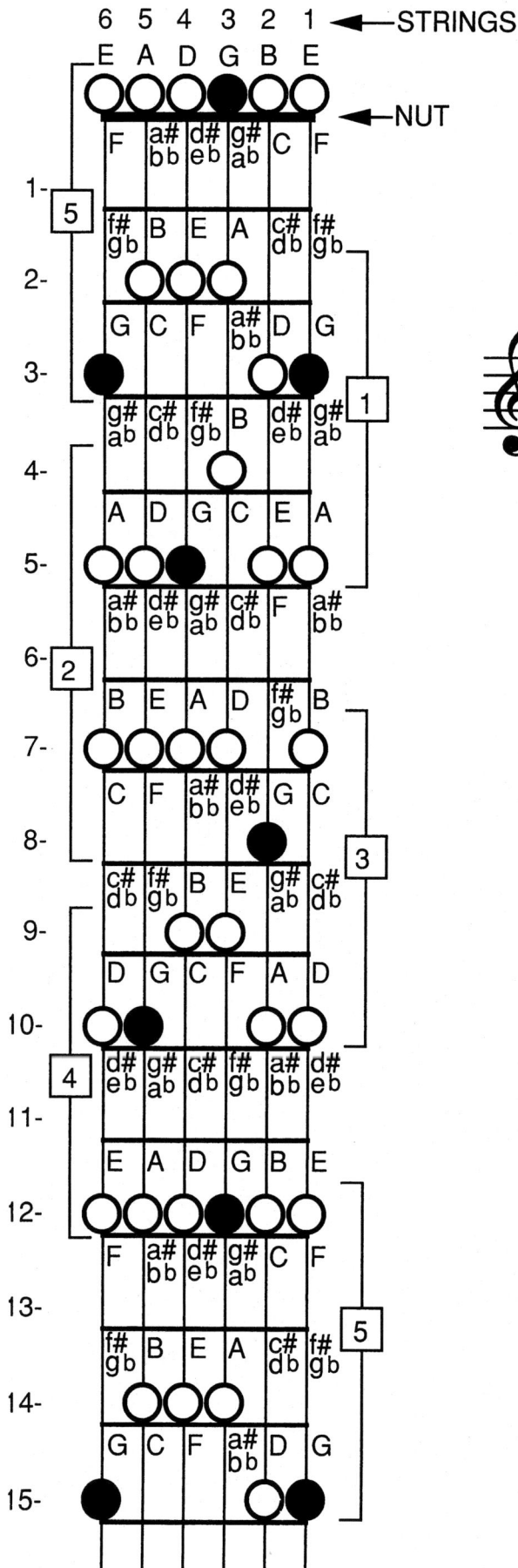

MAJOR PENTATONIC

1-2-3-5-6

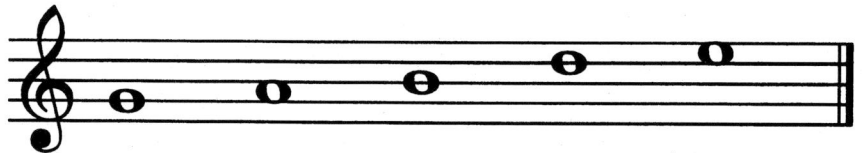

ALTERNATE NAMES:
none

PRIMARY USE:
The Major Pentatonic is used over major triads, major 7th, major add9, major 9th and unaltered dominant chords such as dom7, dom9 and dom13.

SECONDARY USES:
This scale can be used in a wide variety of different harmonic contexts, although you won't necessarily be starting the scale on the root of the chord.

Chord Type	Note to start scale on
maj9	start scale on chordal 5th
maj13	start scale on chordal 9th
min7	start scale on chordal 3rd
min9	start scale on chordal 7th
min13	start scale on chordal 11th
sus7	start scale on either 4th or 7th
dom7#9	start scale on #9 of chord
dom7#5#9	start scale an augmented 4th above chordal root.

PENTATONIC MAJOR

1

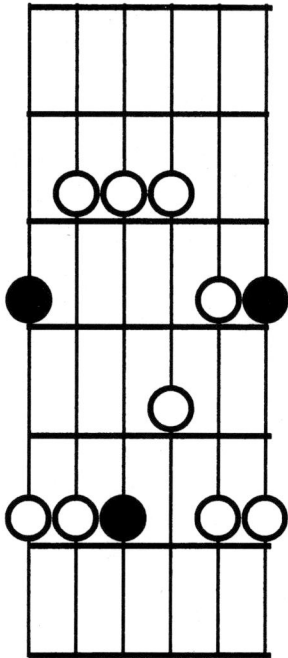

2

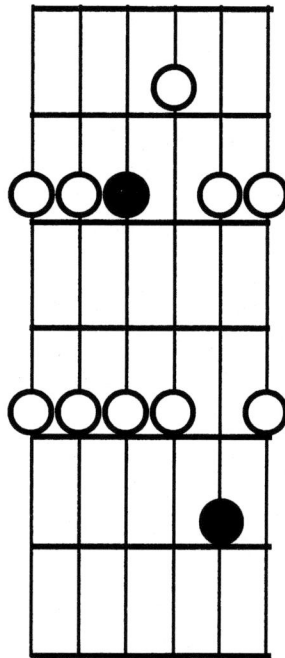

3

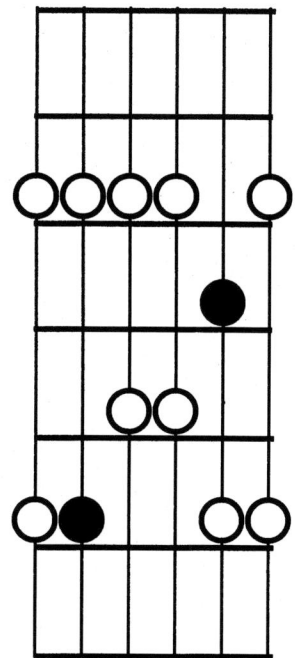

4

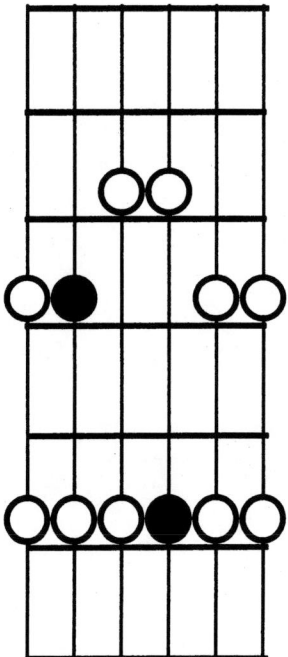

5

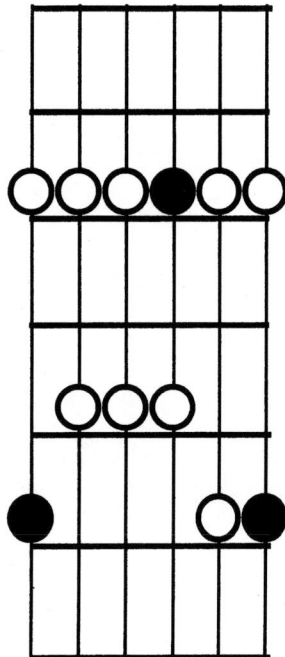

54

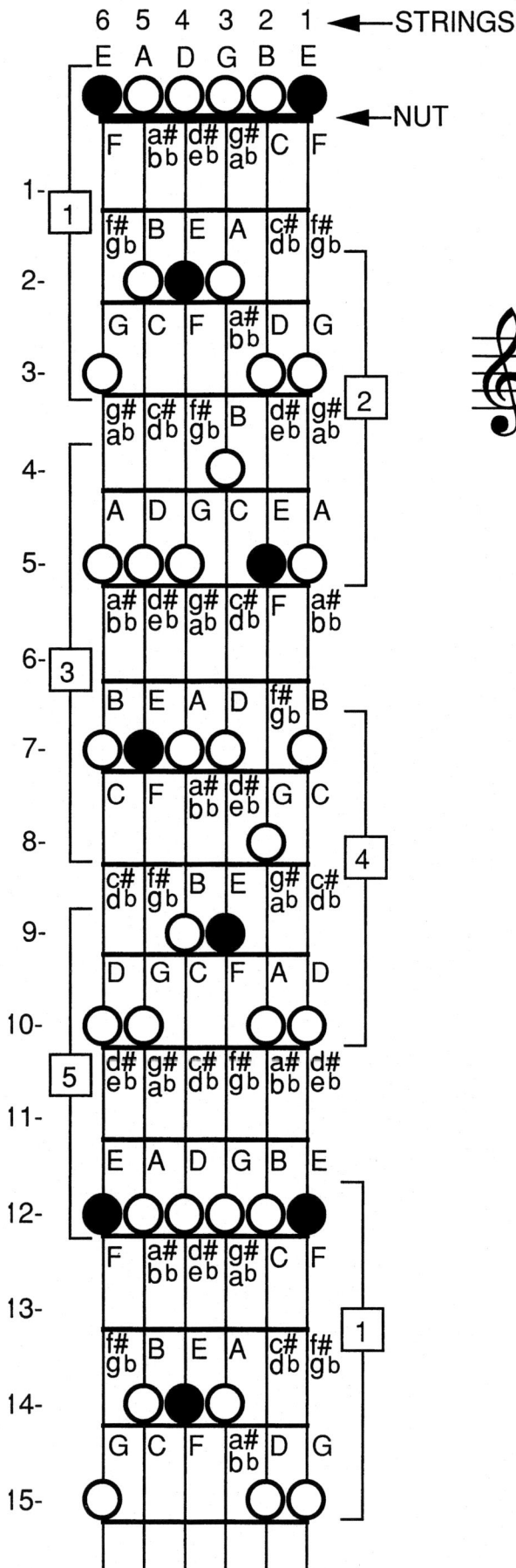

MINOR PENTATONIC

1-b3-4-5-b7

ALTERNATE NAMES:
The Rock Scale or sometimes mistakenly, the Blues scale.

PRIMARY USE:
The Minor Pentatonic scale is used by Rock musicians frequently. As its name implies, it's a minor scale, so it works well over any type of unaltered minor chord. It can also work well over major triads, two-note 5th's (these are also called "power chords"), and nearly any type of dominant chord, both altered and unaltered.

SECONDARY USES:
There are many other uses for this scale, like there is for the major pentatonic.

Chord Type	Note to start scale on
min7	start scale on chordal 5th
min9	start scale on chordal 5th
min11	start scale on 5th or 9th
min6	start scale on chordal 9th

PENTATONIC MINOR

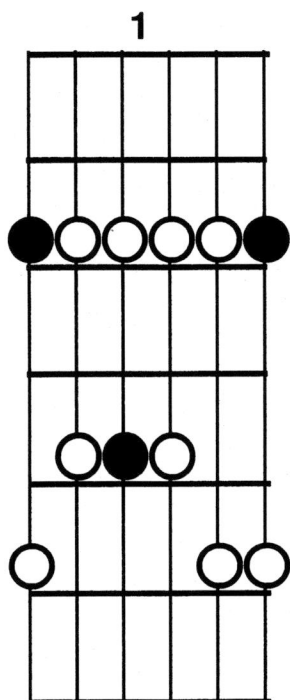

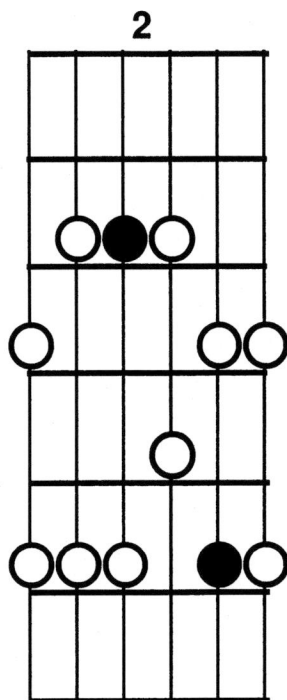

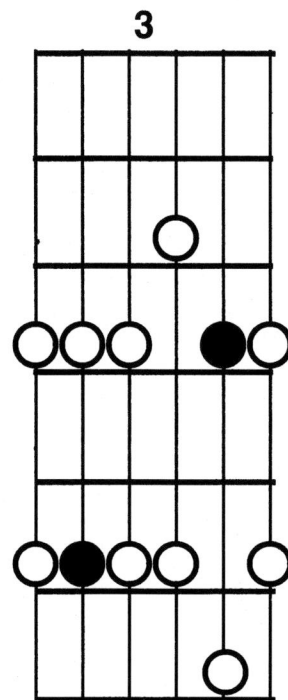

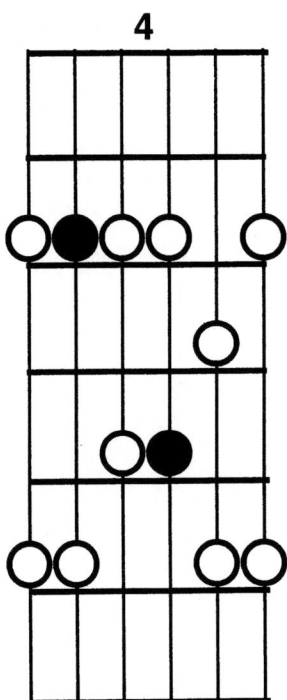

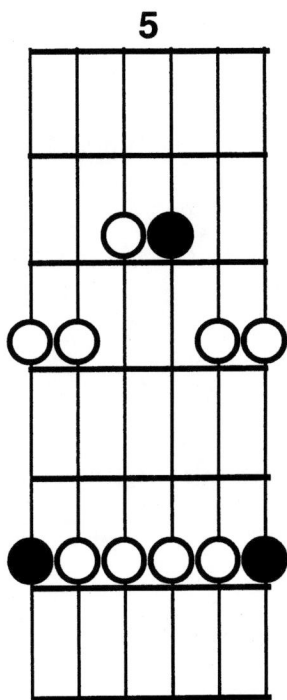

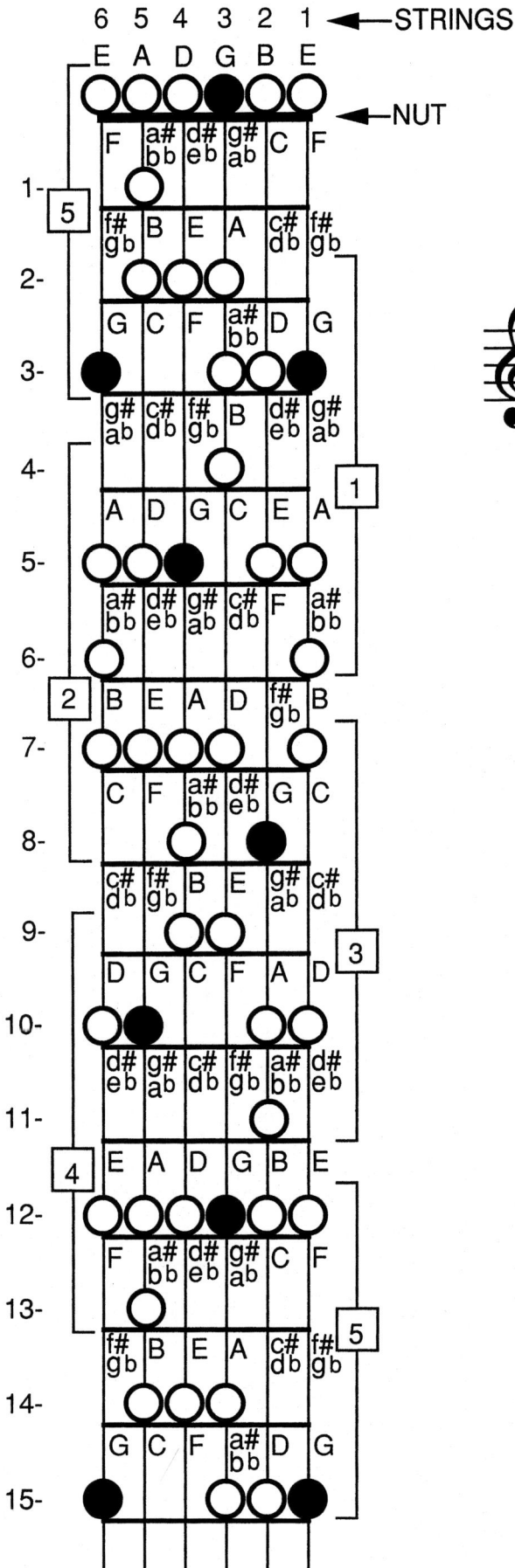

BLUES TYPE A (major)

1-2-b3-♮3-5-6

ALTERNATE NAMES:
none

PRIMARY USE:
This specialized blues scale is not used as frequently as the Type B blues scale, which has a darker sound. This scale is closer to the Major Pentatonic scale, but has a lowered 3rd, which gives it a bluesy sound. Use this scale over major triads, maj6 and unaltered dominant chords such as dom7, dom9 and dom13. The lowered 3rd may sound dissonant against a major chord, so use this note as a passing tone.

EXAMPLE:
Use this scale over any of the following chords: G, G6, Gm6, G7, G9 and G13.

BLUES TYPE (A)

1

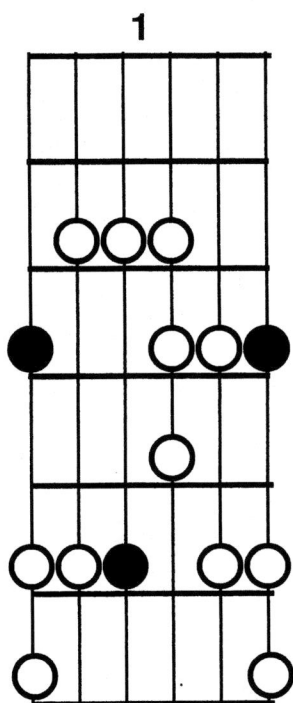

2

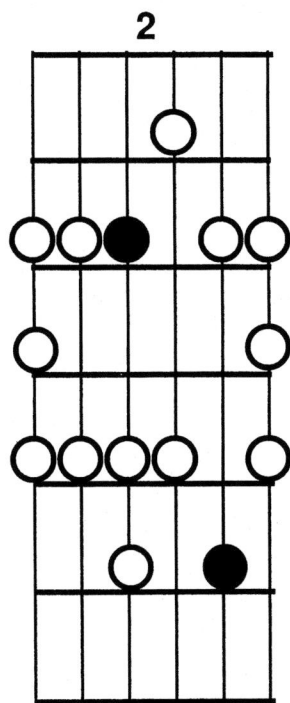

3

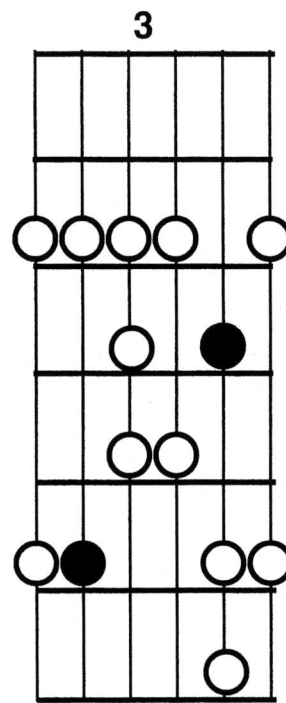

4

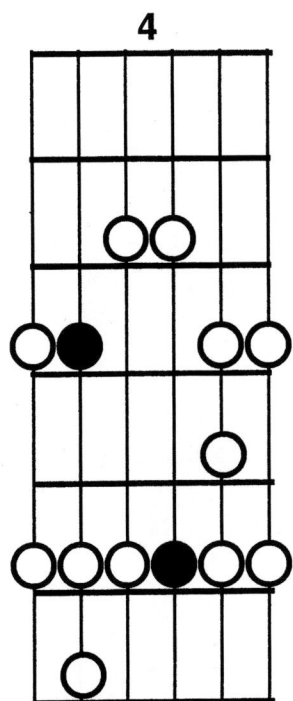

5

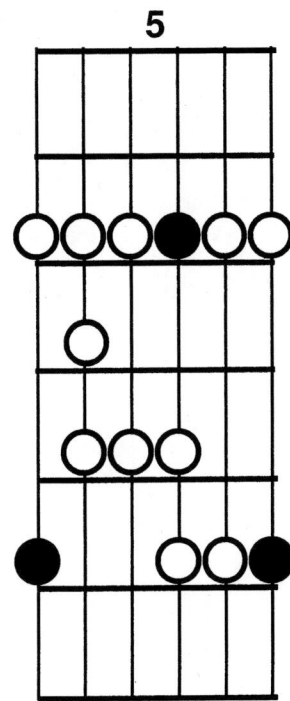

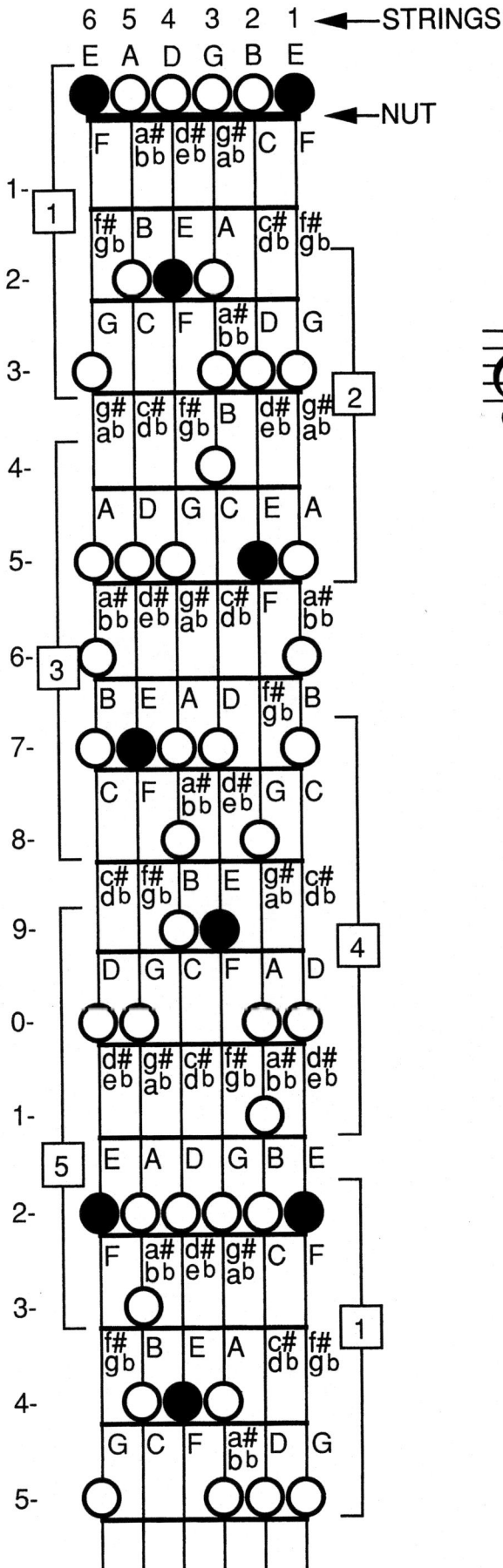

BLUES TYPE (B)

1-b3-4-#4-5-b7

ALTERNATE NAMES:
The Blues scale.

PRIMARY USE:
This is the most frequently heard scale in all of pop, rock and jazz music. It can be used over just about any type of chord imaginable. It is usually played over "power chords", maj triads, unaltered min chords, and all types of dominant chords, both altered and unaltered.

EXAMPLE:
Use this scale anytime you want a bluesy sound. It can be used over any of the following chords whose roots are E. E7, E9, Esus7, E13, E7b5, E7#9, E, Emaj6, Emaj7, Em, Em6, Em7, Em9 and Em11. This is not an exhaustive list, but a starting point.

BLUES TYPE (B)

1

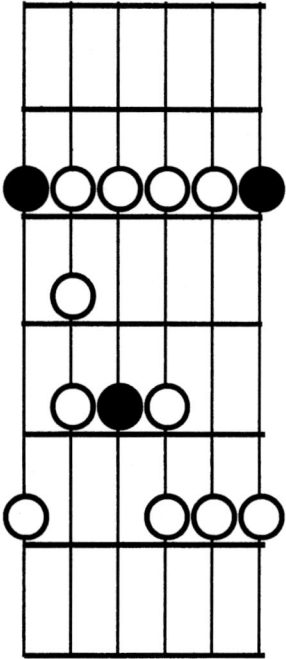

2

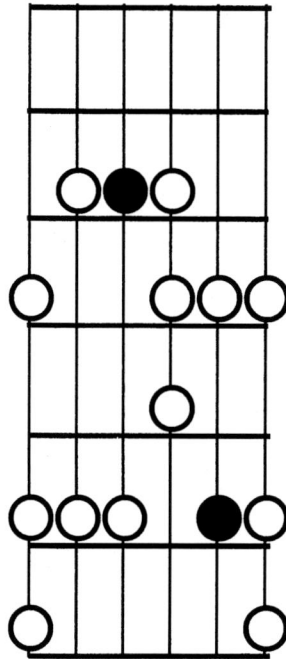

3

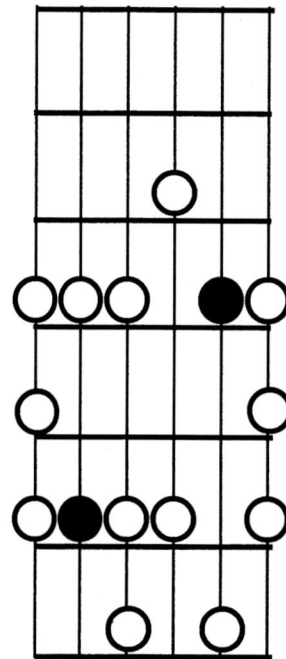

4

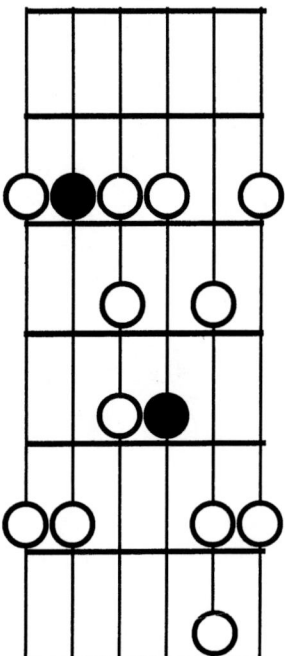

5

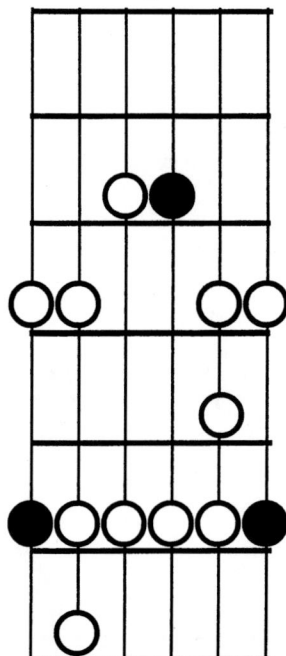

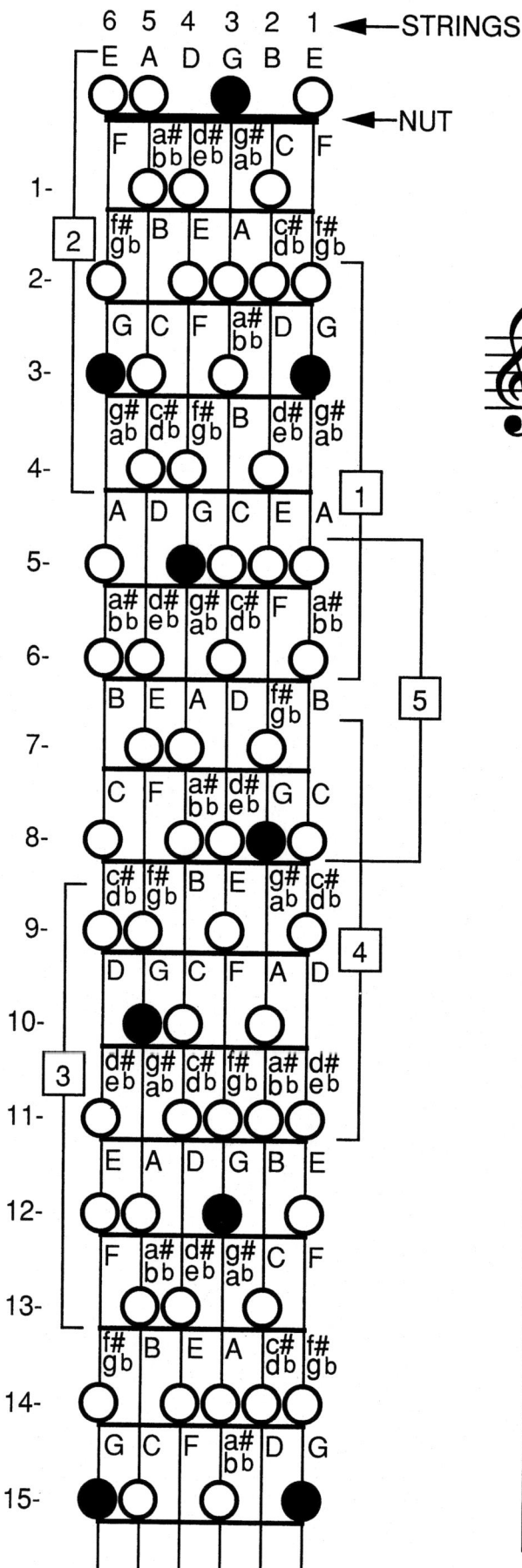

DIMINISHED W/H

1-2-b3-4-b5-b6-♮6-7

ALTERNATE NAMES:
Double diminished scale

PRIMARY USES:
The Diminished scale has only 2 modes. One which begins with a whole-step (the one shown here) and one which begins with a half-step. The one shown here, refered to as Whole/half, is used over diminished 7th chords. Because the dim7 chord repeats itself exactly every 3 frets (a minor 3rd interval), you can use one scale position to play over 4 different diminished 7th chords. These chords all contain exactly the same pitches, but are spelled differently.

EXAMPLE:
Use this scale over Gdim7, Bbdim7, C#dim7 and Edim7.

NOTE:
This scale pattern repeats itseld every 3 frets, or every minor 3rd. Notice also that this is an 8 note scale. Most scales in this book have 7 notes.

DIMINISHED W/H

1

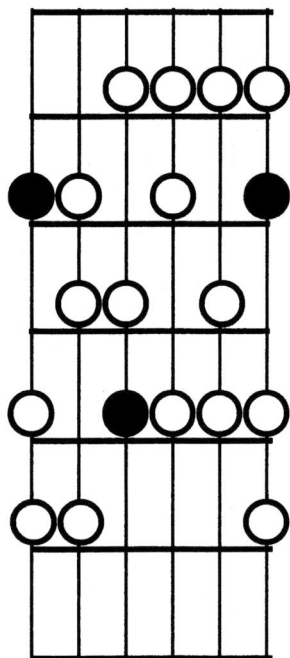

2

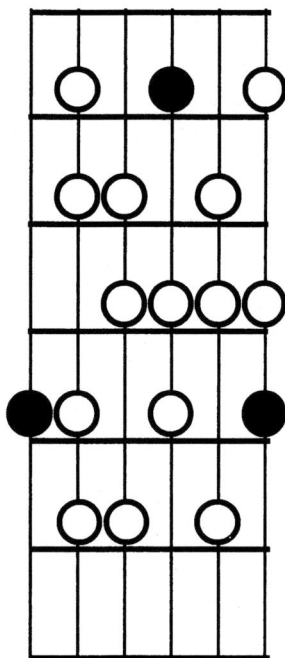

3

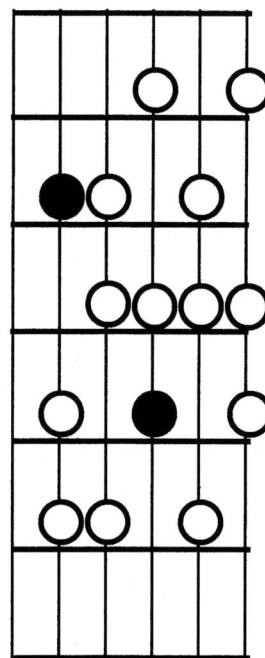

4

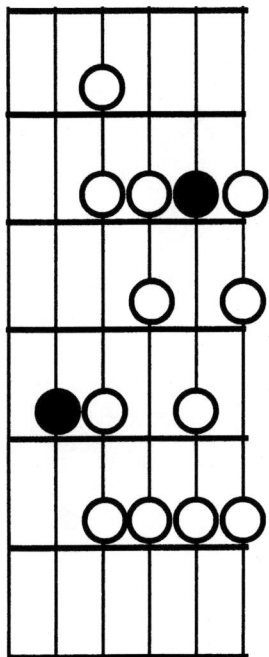

5

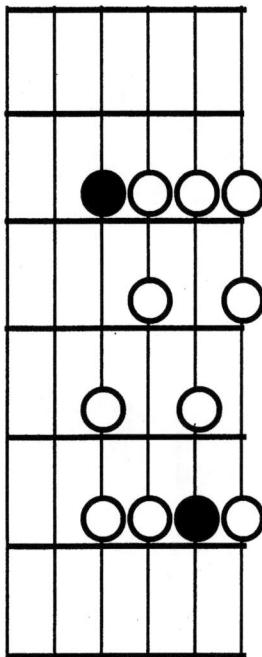

*Here are a variety of different patterns which emerge from this scale.

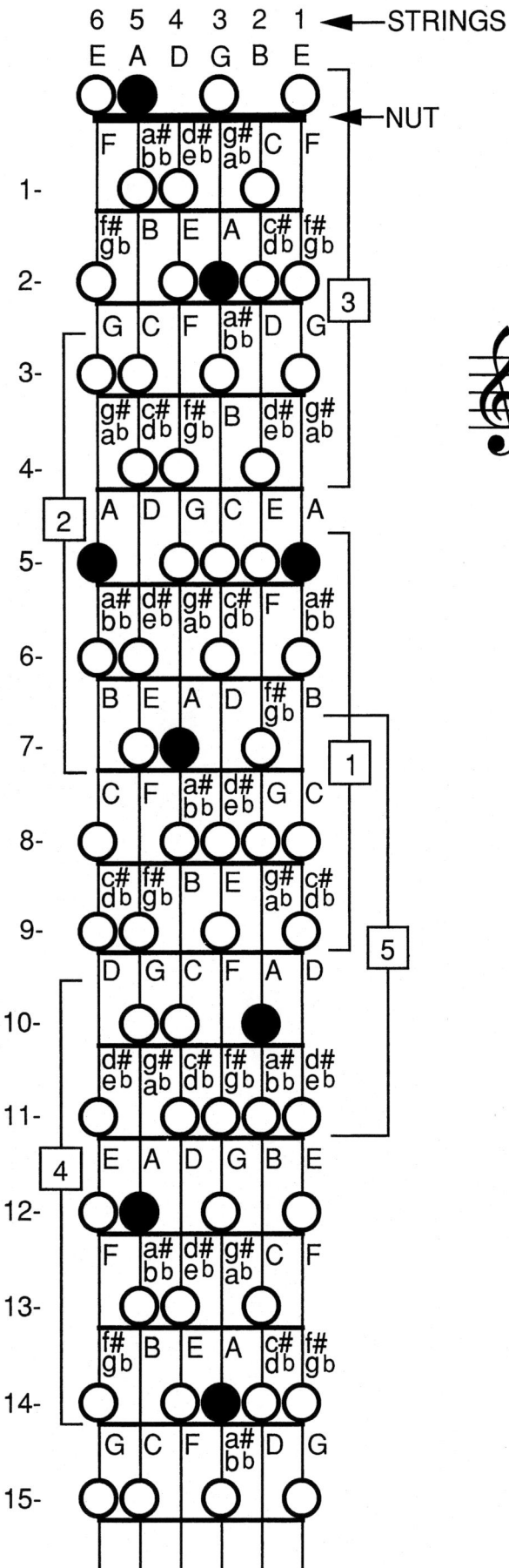

DIMINISHED H/W

1-b2-b3-♮3-#4-5-6-b7

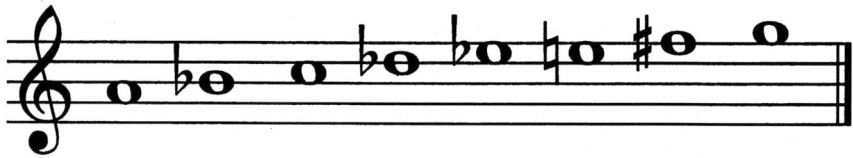

ALTERNATE NAMES:
none

PRIMARY USES:
The Diminished scale has only 2 modes. One which begins with a whole-step and one which begins with a half-step., which is shown here. The one shown here, refered to as the Half/Whole, is used over dominant 7th chords, especially those with a b9, #9, b5 and #11. It is also possible to use this scale over any unaltered dominant chord. When you do this, you're superimposing an altered scale sound over an unaltered harmony. The marriage may be unpleasant to some, but is often done by Jazz musicians.

EXAMPLE:
Use this scale over A7, A9, A13, A7b9, A7#9, A7b5, A7#11 and A7b5b9.

NOTE:
This scale repeats itself every 3 frets.

DIMINISHED H/W

1

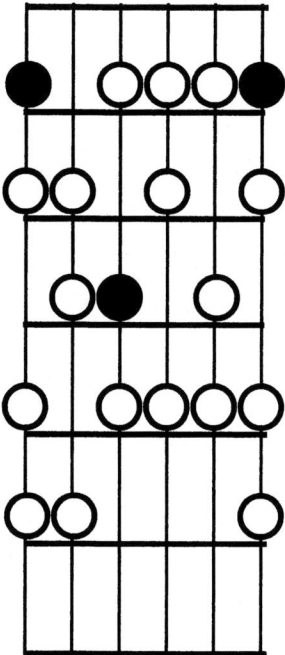

2

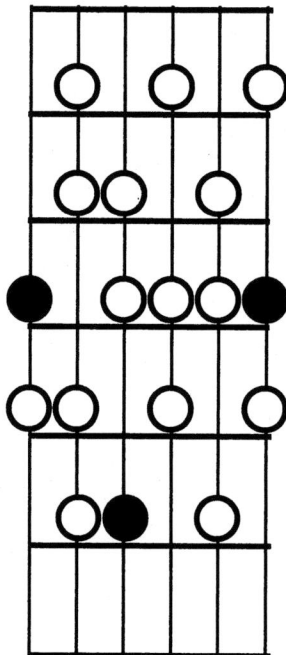

3

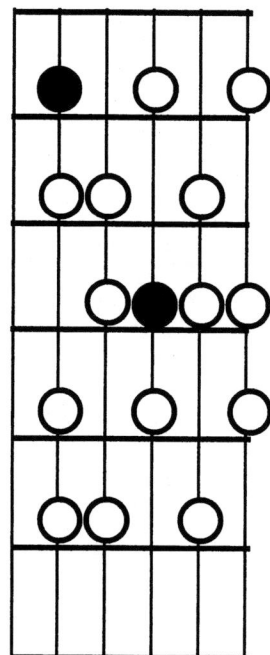

4

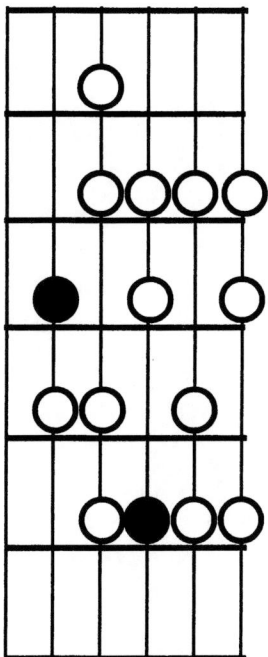

5

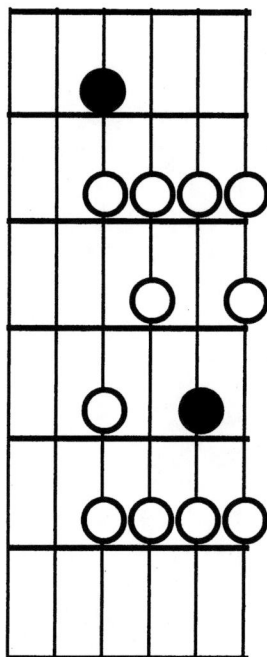

*Here are a variety of different patterns which emerge from this scale.

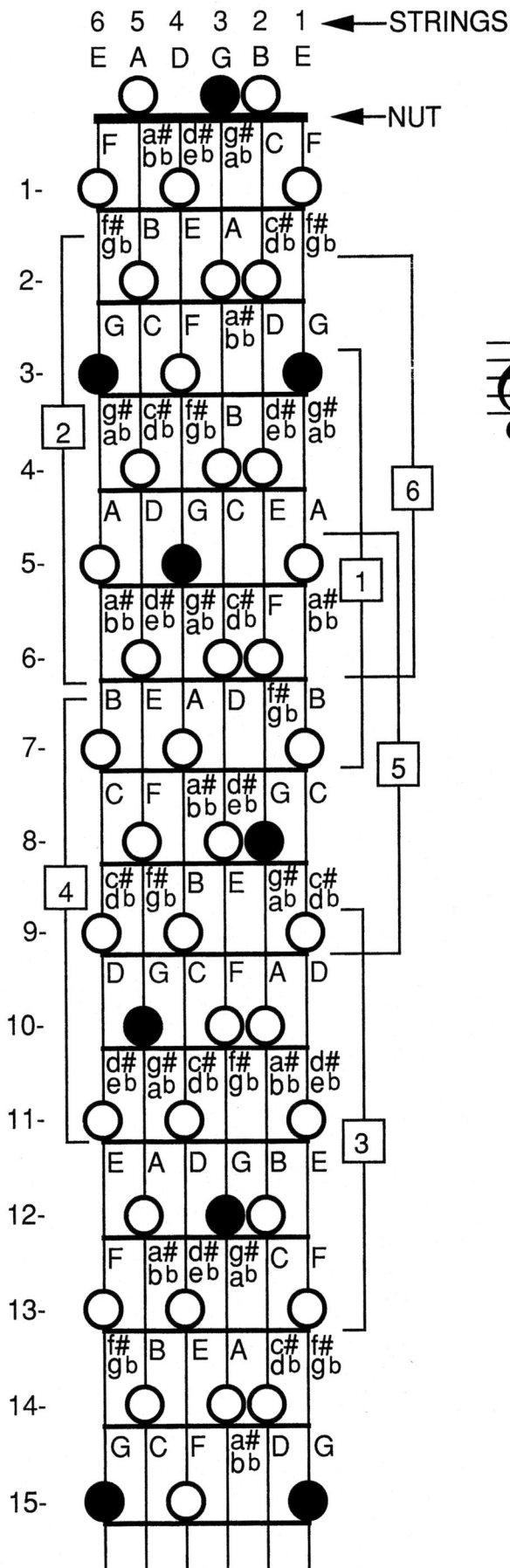

WHOLE TONE

1-2-3-#4-#5-b7

ALTERNATE NAMES:
Augmented scale

PRIMARY USES:
The whole tone scale is a six note scale. It's construction couldn't be simpler; every note is one whole step apart. Because of this, there are two modes possible and they both have exactly the same fingering. If you build a whole tone scale from C, you'd have C-D-E-F#-G#-A#. If you build one from C#, you'd have C#-D#-E#-G-A-B. These two modes of this scale cover every possible note on the guitar.

You can begin a whole tone scale from any note in the scale. Because the whole tone scale is made up of only whole steps, it doesn't really have a tonic or root sound. You must give it a sense of direction through phrasing. This is the type of sound a film composer might use to convey insanity or chaos. Use this scale over dominant chords, especially those with a #4, b5, #5 and #11.

EXAMPLE:
Use the G whole tone scale over G7, G7b5, G7#5, G7#11, G9#11, G9b5, G9#5, G13b5, G13#11 and G13#5.

WHOLE TONE

*Here are six different possible fingerings for the whole tone scale.

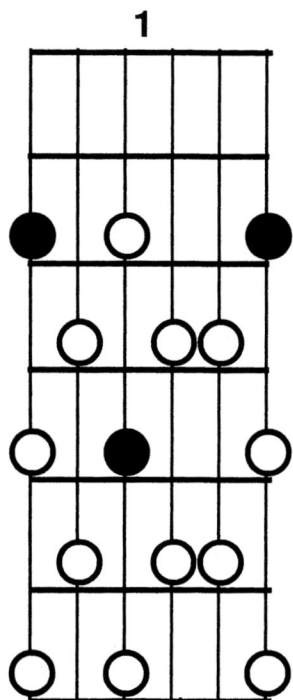

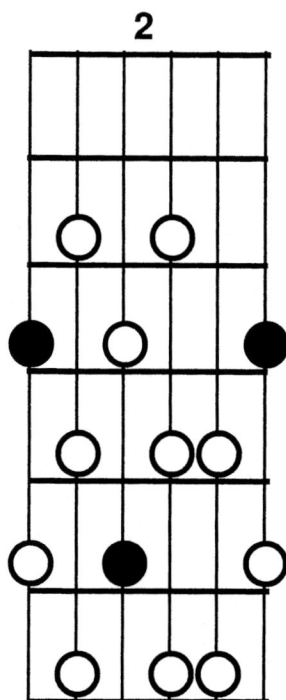

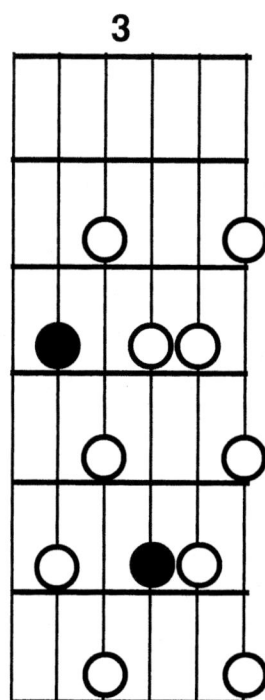

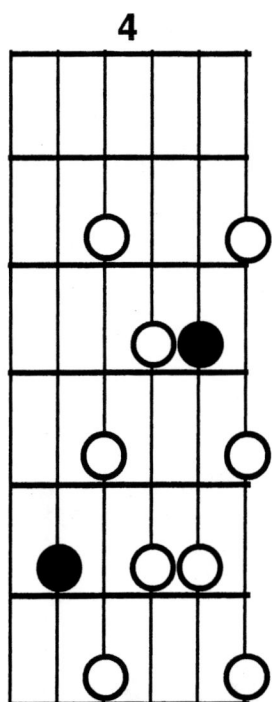

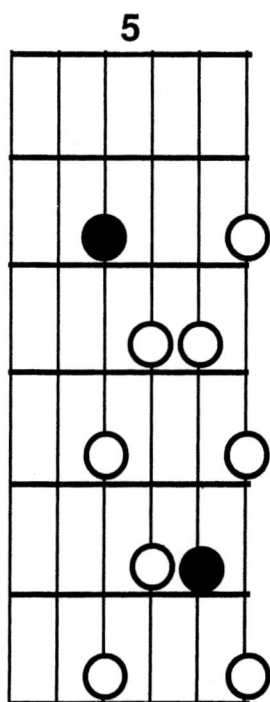

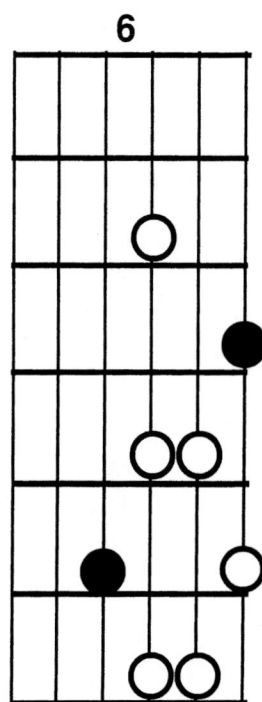

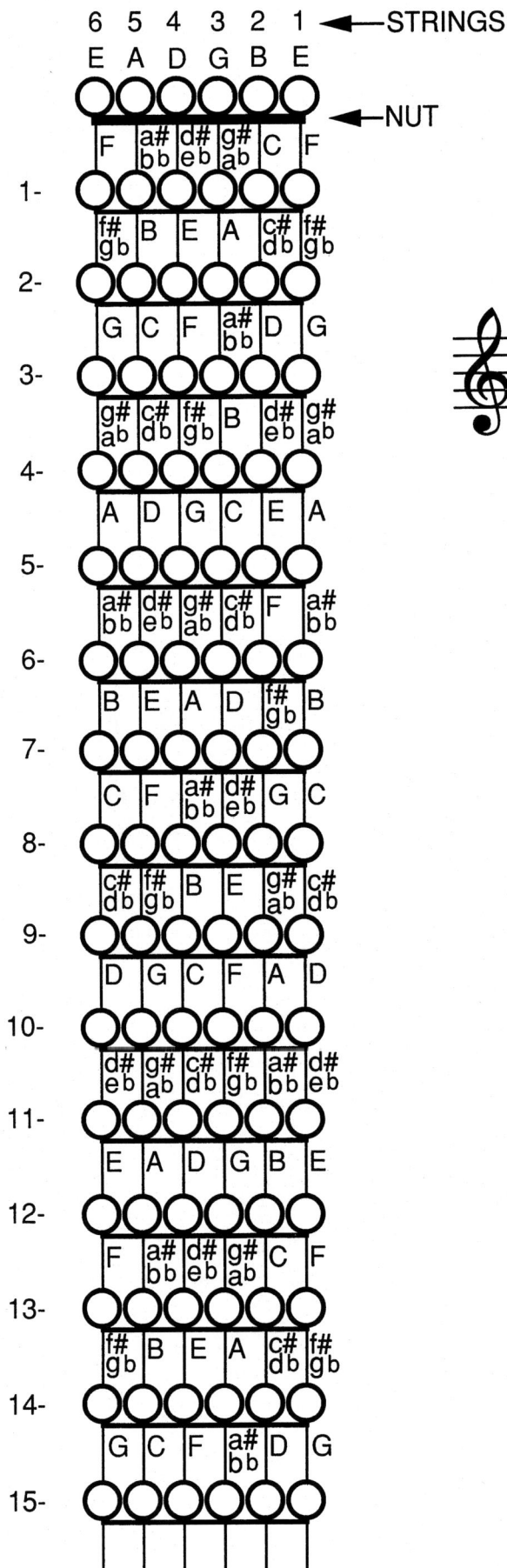

STRINGS

6 5 4 3 2 1
E A D G B E

← NUT

CHROMATIC

1-b2-2-b3-3-4-b5-5-b6-6-b7-7

ALTERNATE NAMES:
none

PRIMARY USES:
The chromatic scale contains every possible note commonly found in Western Music. It contains all of the the scales found in this book. By itself, it's not terribly useful except perhaps as a warmup exercise. I do use it occassionally as a means of interjecting some "chaos" into my soloing. I've also found that you can use this scale over a diminished 7th chord. This is also the scale I fall into when I'm lost. I pull out of it when I can get a fix on which scale I really should be in. A more musical way of putting it would be to say that I use this scale to "transition" from one idea to another.

CHROMATIC

*Here are a variety of different patterns which emerge from this scale.

Two ways to finger the ascending chromatic scale. Play these pitches in the order shown inside each circle.

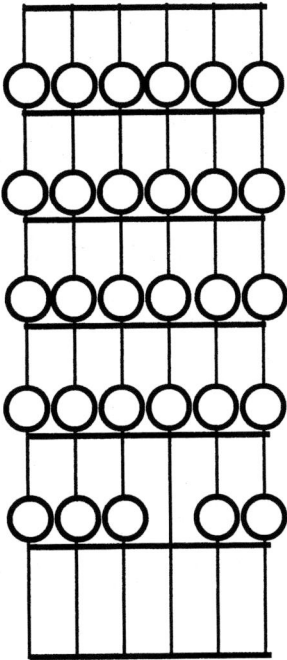

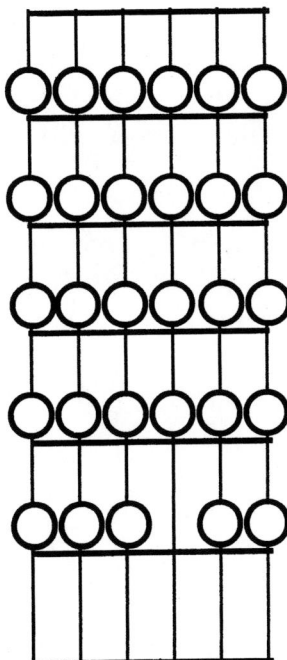

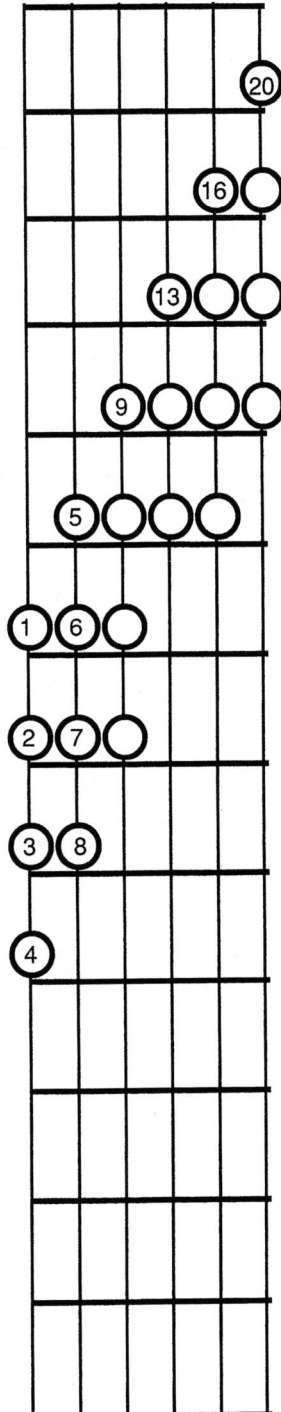

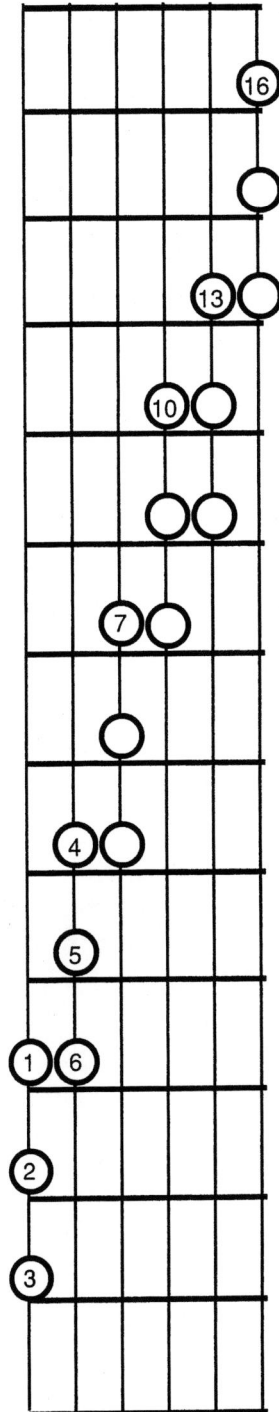

CHORD/SCALE RELATIONSHIPS

The following list of chords and scales is intended to show some of the possible uses for the scales shown in this book. These scale choices are the ones frequently used when improvising over the chords shown to the left. The scale choices include primary and secondary uses.

It's common to begin certain scales on a note which is contained within the chord over which you wish to improvise. This is a clear use of the scale in a secondary function. For example, it's possible to superimpose a minor pentatonic scale over a chord belonging to the major chord family, whose root is the 3rd of the chord. If you use Cmaj7 as an example, then you must begin the minor pentatonic scale based on an E note, which is the chordal 3rd of the Cmaj7 chord. (The formula for a maj7 chord is 1-3-5-7, or C-E-G-B.) What you are accomplishing by beginning a minor pentatonic on the chordal 3rd is to play a scale whose notes consist of E-G-A-B-D. When these tones are heard in the context of a Cmaj7, the resulting sound is of a Cmaj6/9. This is so, because the pitches of the E min pentatonic are the 3rd, 5th, 6th, 7th and 9th of the C major scale. Our ears hear the chord and the scale pitches in a summing process so that the total effect of the chord and scale produce a sound which is greater than each individual sound or either the scale or the chord. It's also to play a minor pentatonic whose root is based on the chordal 7th of a major7th chord. This would mean that you'd be superimposing a B minor pentatonic over a Cmaj7. The tones which are produced by using this scale are: B-D-E-F#-A. These tones are the 7th, 9th, 3rd, #4 and 6th of the C major scale. This type of superimposition will produce a Lydian sound because of the raised 4th.

Most people think that to improvise over a jazz tune you need to play a different scale over each chord. This is not necessarily so, although some people are skilled enough to do this. What actually occurs is a grouping of chords within a key or tonal center. Once you can determine that a given series of chords belongs to a key, then you can play one scale over this series. There are times when you will change scales depending on the function of a chord within a progression. Determining chord functions is beyond the scope of this book. If you're interested in understanding this topic further (and you must be if you want to solo on jazz tunes), then consult my book called INTRODUCTION TO CHORD THEORY.

The scale choices recommended here are based on the assumption that all chords are functioning as tonic chords. In other words, the scale will work over the chord(s) listed, but may not work if you add a different type of chord not listed as being one of the ones in the left hand column (assuming you're playing the proper root).

CHORD TYPE	SCALE CHOICES
maj triads, maj6, maj7 maj6/9, maj9, maj add9	1- maj pentatonic 2- maj pentatonic on 2nd of chord 3- maj pentatonic on 4th of chord 4- maj pentatonic on 5th of chord 5- min pentatonic on 3rd of chord 6- min pentatonic on 7th of chord 7- Ionian mode 8- Lydian mode 9- 6th mode of Harmonic minor 10- Blues (type A and B)
maj7b5, maj7#4, maj7#11	1- Lydian mode 2- 3rd mode of Harmonic minor 3- 6th mode of Harmonic minor 4- min pentatonic on 7th of chord
maj7#5	1- 3rd mode of Melodic minor (also known as Lydian-augmented) 2- 3rd mode of Harmonic minor 3- 6th mode of Harmonic minor
suspended 2, suspended 4 suspended 7 suspended 9 suspended 13	1- Ionian mode 2- minor pentatonic on 2nd of chord 3- Phrygian mode 4- Mixolydian mode 5- 5th mode of Harmonic minor 6- minor pentatonic on root of chord 7- Blues (type B)
min triads, min7, min9 min add9	1- Dorian mode 2- Aeolian mode 3- minor pentatonic on chord root 4- minor pentatonic on 5th of chord 5- Blues (type B) 6- Phrygian mode 7- Harmonic minor on chord root 8- 4th mode of Harmonic minor 9- Melodic minor on chord root 10- 2nd mode of Melodic minor 11- Major pentatonic on 3rd of chord 12- diminished (W/H) starting on chord root

CHORD TYPE	SCALE CHOICES
min6, min6/9, min6/7, min13	1- Dorian mode 2- Minor pentatonic on chord root 3- Minor pentatonic on 2nd of chord 4- Melodic minor on chord root 5- 2nd mode of Melodic minor 6- Blues (type B) 7- Major pentatonic on 4th of chord
min11	1- Dorian mode 2- Aeolian mode 3- Minor pentatonic on chord root 4- Minor pentatonic on 5th of chord 5- Harmonic minor on chord root 6- Blues (type B)
min#7	1- Melodic minor on chord root 2- Harmonic minor on chord root 3- Whole tone on 7th of chord 4- 4th mode of Harmonic minor
min7b5	1- Locrian mode 2- Blues (type B) 3- 2nd mode of Harmonic minor 4- Harmonic minor on 7th of chord 5- Melodic minor on 3rd of chord 6- 6th mode of Melodic minor 7- 7th mode of Melodic minor 8- Diminished (W/H) on chord root
min9b5	1- 6th mode of Melodic minor
dom7, dom9, dom13	1- Mixolydian mode 2- Major pentatonic on chord root 3- Minor pentatonic on chord root 4- Whole tone on chord root 5- Diminished (H/W) on chord root 6- Blues (both types)
dom7b9(sus4)	1- Phrygian mode 2- 5th Mode of Harmonic minor

CHORD TYPE	SCALE CHOICES
dom7b5, dom7#4, dom7#11	1- Whole tone on chord root 2- 4th mode of Melodic minor 3- 7th mode of Melodic minor 4- 5th mode of Harmonic minor
dom7#5, augmented 7, augmented triad, dom9#5	1- Whole tone on chord root 2- 5th mode of Melodic minor 3- 7th mode of Melodic minor 4- 4th mode of Melodic minor
dom7b9	1- Diminished (H/W) on chord root 2- Chromatic 3- Harmonic minor on chord root 4- 5th mode of Harmonic minor 5- 7th mode of Melodic minor
dom7#9	1- Blues (type B) 2- Diminished (H/W) on chord root 3- Minor pentatonic on chord root 4- Major pentatonic on 3rd of chord 5- 5th mode of Harmonic minor 6- 7th mode of Melodic minor
dom7b9#9	1- Diminished (H/W) on chord root 2- 7th mode of Harmonic minor 3- 7th mode of Melodic minor
altered chords dom7b5b9, dom7b5#9, dome7#5b9, dom9#5#9	1- 7th mode of melodic minor 2- Minor pentatonic on b3 of chord 3- Major pentatonic on #4 of chord 4- Chromatic scale
suspended 4, sus7, sus9, sus11, sus13	1- Mixolydian mode on chord root 2- Phrygian mode on chord root 3- Minor pentatonic on 2nd of chord 4- Minor pentatonic on 5th of chord 5- Major pentatonic on 4th of chord 6- Major pentatonic on 7th of chord
diminished triad, diminished 7	1- Diminished (W/H) on chord root 2- Chromatic 3- 7th mode of Harmonic minor